WHAT TO SAY AND WHEN TO SHUT UP

Praise for the book

'A user-friendly guide for navigating difficult situations and discussions that we come across both in our professional and personal lives...definitely a must read.'

Prof Praveen Kopalle
Professor of Marketing and Chair, Marketing Department, Tuck School of Business, Dartmouth College

'Even as I talk to my patients, I make it a point to look into their eyes, touch them and in that gesture see the amazing power of healing set in. Speech carries not just the power of the word; it touches the healer within. An apt book.'

Dr Devi Shetty
Chairman, Narayan Hrudayalaya Hospitals

'A good teacher helps you understand and empowers you to be effective. Rakesh Godhwani does exactly that in this insightful book on the art of persuasion.'

Prof M.V. Rajeev Gowda
Member of Parliament, Rajya Sabha

'A book on a compelling subject. The art of effective communication, both speaking and listening, can make or break careers of talented professionals. All aspiring leaders and entrepreneurs should read this.'

Samir Kumar
Managing Director, Inventus Advisory Services India

'In today's globalized world, impactful communication is a critical factor for managers and leaders to succeed in business.

Rakesh's book, written in a very simple style, is a very practical guidebook to nurture and sharpen capabilities in this area. This book will be especially useful for a lot of marketing and communication experts.'

Saugata Gupta
Managing Director and CEO, Marico Ltd.

'Communication and persuasion skills in students and young professionals is a very important topic for the industry and I am glad that finally, someone from India has given this subject its due credit. It will be good if all colleges, through this book, build this critical expertise among the students. The industry will greatly benefit by having a workforce which can communicate effectively.'

R. Chandrasekaran
Executive Vice Chairman, Cognizant India and Chairman, NASSCOM

'People are increasingly interested in knowing "why something needs to be done" versus being told "what they need to do". In today's corporate world, leaders will be effective only if they are able to persuade or convince others to follow. Adopting Godhwani's simple yet powerful 6 element framework will help readers master the elusive and uncommon art of persuasive communications.'

Das Narayandas
Senior Associate Dean, HBS Publishing and Executive Education
James J. Hill Professor of Business Administration
Harvard Business School

WHAT TO SAY AND WHEN TO SHUT UP

Rakesh Godhwani

PENGUIN BUSINESS
An imprint of Penguin Random House

PENGUIN BUSINESS

USA | Canada | UK | Ireland | Australia
New Zealand | India | South Africa | China | Singapore

Penguin Business is an imprint of the Penguin Random House group of companies whose addresses can be found at global.penguinrandomhouse.com

Published by Penguin Random House India Pvt. Ltd
4th Floor, Capital Tower 1, MG Road,
Gurugram 122 002, Haryana, India

Penguin Random House India

First published by Random House India 2014
Published in Portfolio by Penguin Random House India 2019
Published in Penguin Business by Penguin Random House India 2024

10 9 8 7 6 5 4

ISBN 9788184006025

Typeset in Adobe Garamond by Saanvi Graphics, Noida
Printed at Manipal Technologies Limited, India

www.penguin.co.in

FSC www.fsc.org MIX Paper | Supporting responsible forestry FSC® C043100

This is a legitimate digitally printed version of the book and therefore might not have certain extra finishing on the cover.

To Simran, Kian, and Aarohi

Contents

PART 3

Part 1

Chapter 1

This Book

The problem

I was sitting in a plush room, in a swanky resort situated in the suburbs of the city, waiting for my turn to address an audience of around two hundred people who worked for a company that made parts for cars. This was their Quarterly Business Meeting. I had been invited as an external speaker to give a motivational speech on communication for leaders, inspired by my own career and my last book *Seek: Finding Your True Calling*. The CEO of the company was giving an overall update on the company's performance. Soon my friend, the head of the HR, sent me a small post-it note informing the delay for my speech. It had been pushed to the third slot, immediately before the lunch hour. Earlier I had been allotted the second slot, just after the tea break at 11:15 am. I was obviously not happy with the change in my turn. But what could I do? So I settled down at the back of the room and bided my time.

The CEO of the group was an alumnus of an Ivy League college, a corporate veteran, and possessed excessive knowledge on the new car accessories that were the rage. While his speech was still going strong, I glanced at my watch—11:30 am. He still had some 72 slides to go through and I could already feel the effect of his speech by looking around me. People were busy WhatsApp-ing each other about how boring the speech was. I managed to peek into the mobile of the person sitting next to me and it read—'Shoot him or shoot me'. I squirmed in my seat.

It was still slide 34 at 11:45. Even I was irritated. The only person enjoying the talk was the speaker himself. The other person who was mildly interested was the person who was to speak next. Finally the emcee of the event gestured to the CEO—'time for tea break'. The CEO apologized for not realizing the time and, to the relief of the audience, promised to end it in two minutes. As to be expected, everyone was suddenly awake from their slumber to welcome the end of the CEO's seemingly endless speech. But to everyone's grief, the CEO did not live up to his promise. Those two minutes turned out to be much longer. He was in no mood to stop apparently. It took another reminder from the emcee before he said, 'Thank you. I hope you realize how important you all are to this organization. Any questions?' Thoughts of tea were instantly banished.

Remember when we were in school and desperately waiting for the bell to toll for the lunch hour? And remember, when the teacher would end the class at 12:59 pm—just a minute before the lunch hour, and would ask 'any questions?' There would invariably be an irritating Chatur Mahalingam or Chatura Mahalingam who had to ask a question right then. The whole class would go, 'Oh nooooooo! Ahhhhhh, awwwwwww' and feel like lynching Chatur/Chatura. We felt similarly that day. No sooner had the CEO asked for questions that one Chatur stood up. 'Hello Jack! I am Chatur and I work in this department. I want to tell you how proud I am to be a part of this organization. I loved your talk....' And he went on in this vague vein for some minutes. The audience was visibly fidgety now. The CEO said, 'Chatur, what's your question?' And Chatur said, 'I am coming to that...' and went on for another minute. Finally Chatur asked, 'Why haven't you paid any bonus this year? All your slides showed the amount of money we made and how well we are doing. So why don't you share profits with employees?' Suddenly, everyone laughed. Some people even clapped and supported Chatur. The CEO was red-faced. He forced a smile and hastily said, 'Let's discuss this over tea.'

The break lasted 20 minutes. The next speaker had not learned any lessons from the previous speaker and again showed 50 slides, ending his talk around 1:30 pm. Naturally the audience had had enough by then and was in no mood for another presentation. They were hungry too. Realizing that hunger pangs and speeches did not make a good combination, I whispered to the HR head, 'Do you want to push my talk post lunch?' 'No. We have a packed agenda for the afternoon,' he said. 'There is no point in doing this talk. The audience is switched off and annoyed. I suggest you break for lunch. And cancel my talk,' I told him. He insisted, however, that I stay and finish my talk before lunch. He was a close friend; I couldn't let him down.

So I readied myself to the challenge of keeping the drowsy and hungry audience interested in my speech. I walked up to the podium and announced, 'I need a volunteer with a stop watch.' One person waved his phone. 'Thank you,' I said. By then, everyone was quiet. I asked the person to set his stop watch to 5 minutes, 'I promise I will speak for exactly 5 minutes or less. If I exceed by even a second, I will pay a fine of Rs 100 to each of you in this room because I know that you all are hungry and the only person standing between lunch and you is me. Ready?' The person with the stopwatch grinned and nodded. There was pin-drop silence in the room.

'Friends, I thank Ajit and Ramesh for inviting me. More importantly, I thank all of you for being a wonderful audience. Like the rest of you in this room, I am also an engineer. I enjoyed making laptops and cell phones like how you enjoy making cars. But along the way I found that I enjoy teaching much more than making computers. So one day, I took the Plunge and now I work at my alma mater IIM Bangalore as the head of the alumni office and as an adjunct faculty. I am here to give all of you a very simple message—if you love doing something and can do it without getting tired, then make it your full time job. You will be much more successful. So here are three simple ways on how you too can *Seek* your true calling…'

The audience seemed to be really listening to what I was saying. I went on to illustrate the three points with anecdotes, stopped at 4 minutes 32 seconds, and got a round of applause. At lunch, many of the members of the audience came to me and congratulated me on my short and crisp speech. I was really overwhelmed.

That night, my LinkedIn account was flooded with requests from people who had heard my speech. And all I could wonder was how the CEO and the head of sales didn't even realize that they screwed up so badly. Instead of inspiring, they ended up boring the audience, definitely not what they had intended. Both the CEO and the sales head have enviable educational qualifications, but they failed to communicate effectively. Let's find out why.

Frankly speaking, the company made a gross wastage of time—about 600 man hours that day. If the annual turnover of this company is, say USD 10 billion, that's a waste of about USD 3.5 million. Every day, many precious hours are wasted when people fail to take into account that time is money. As part of the audience to such boring speeches and presentations, we are very harsh and show no mercy, but when it comes to taking the stage, we repeat those same mistakes.

I was struck by another thought—the highly inappropriate nature of Chatur's question. How could he ask that question in a full house? Are certain things not meant to be said in private? Besides his profuse rambling, his question was really annoying too. Instead of mocking Chatur however, we need to introspect and fight the Chatur-like elements that most of us carry with us which crop up at the wrong place and at the wrong time. It is necessary to adhere to certain principle while raising questions in such a set up, especially questions which carry potential to undermine the authority of the bosses or credibility of the company.

Anyway, this is just one example of a very corporate setting. Here is another example from an apartment complex residential association email group. One fine Sunday morning, a member living in this apartment complex sent a long email to the entire group of 340 residents. The mail was as follows:

Dear fellow residents,
I am ashamed by the behaviour of some of you. This morning, I saw a dog from one of the 'respectable families' poo near the swimming pool. My child was in that swimming pool and she saw this spectacle. She told me that she does not want to live here and wants to go back to Seattle. And I was shocked. When I returned from USA, I never thought that my daughter would have to go through this ordeal and come home crying. I ask you—don't you have any basic decency? Why would you leave your dogs in the open like this? I want the President to take strict action and throw out this family from this complex.

About 25 seconds later, a response emerged, *Go back to America. We never asked you to come back...*

Soon more responses followed.

The respectable gentleman who sent this mail has flouted many norms of this association. Despite repeatedly requesting him to segregate waste, he never complies. He has invited his guests inside the complex who are encouraged to park their cars in my slot many times. What right does this 'respectable' gentleman have to throw stones at others when he himself is living in a glass house...

The entire group erupted like a house on fire and no one seemed to care about the main issue—the dog that pooped near the pool. In less than an hour, there were a few dozen slanderous emails from every 'respectable' family in the complex. An old gentleman then wrote, *People, this is not the right forum to send such emails. I request the gentleman who started this email to approach the welfare association committee and resolve...* His email was ignored completely and got buried in the venom that kept spouting from other quarters. It was the only sensible mail that day. There were at least 50 families who asked to be deleted from the group list. Finally, the admin of the group blocked all senders and announced, *This is unproductive. I am out of this group....* This embarrassing episode created deep gashes in the relationships of residents. The expat families formed a separate group and boycotted every event from that day. Finally, the welfare association made some rules on what kind of emails would be allowed on the group; some old seasoned people were made to run the committee who bought some sanity in the association. But the harm was done. A friend of mine who lives in that complex later told me, 'We said things which even my young daughter would think twice before uttering. Sometimes we become so insensitive to each other that I wonder—it's amazing how we can behave like this despite all our civilized upbringing and education.'

Conflicts are inevitable in any form of human society. Anger is a curse. When we open our mouths to say something when we are angry, we are bound to damage something. In the heat of the moment, it is difficult to control ourselves. A word spoken from the mouth is like a bullet. Once fired, it will hit its target and do the damage. There is no way to bring back that bullet. In the case illustrated above, it was an email that was sent in anger. It is no different than a conflict which arises when someone parks their car in front of your house and blocks your gate. You go out fuming at this person and in that anger, hurl abuses at him. We behave as if this person has brought a great harm upon us. And we want to correct his behaviour so that he doesn't dare to do it again. The tone of our voice then fuels this fire and the damage is catastrophic. There is a quote that supports this argument. It goes something like this, '10 percent of conflict is due to difference in opinion and 90 percent is due to the wrong tone of voice'.

When I was in college, studying engineering, I witnessed a fight between some friends over a glass of juice. It seems silly in hindsight, but it triggered a big conflict that lasted an entire evening, broke many friendships, and scarred us for life. It all started when we were standing in queue for the evening snack in the cafeteria. It was juice day. One of us had a lab to go to at 4:30 pm. So he just walked up to the front of the queue, picked up a glass, and gulped it down. The people in the queue objected. 'What's your problem? I have a lab and need to hurry,' he said. Now the entire queue ganged up against him and one guy said, 'Did you ask our permission to break the queue? Don't you have basic courtesy?' One guy piped up, 'Is this your father's college?' And that was it... Very soon tempers rose and everything spiraled out of control. This guy was beaten up. He then ran off to round up his set of friends. When they saw his tattered clothes and blood trickling from his face, they got mad. They came down and the next few hours were horrifying. I know it all sounds like a script from a Bollywood potboiler, but that is exactly how it unfolded... People were extricated out from their hideouts. One guy jumped from the balcony in an attempt to escape and broke his leg. And yes, all this over something as insignificant as a glass of juice. When the human mind goes out of control, we completely lose our sense of perspective.

Why did this happen? I think it's complicated but on closer scrutiny, you can discern the causes. There are behavioural issues, communication issues, and many more psychological factors at play here. How I wish life was like a DVD player and I had a remote that could rewind, fast-forward, or pause at certain phases of my life. Let's rewind this incident and go back to that queue. If this guy (who was in a hurry and had a lab to go to) had requested the others in the queue with a smile and in a friendly tone, 'Hey guys, I need to run to the lab. Can I skip the queue and grab a juice. Thank you so much', I bet you nothing would have happened. We all help each other in situations like this. A smile, some polite words, and little bit of courtesy is all it takes to get your work done. But the moment this guy raised his tone and challenged others with words like 'what is your problem?', he unnecessarily provoked them and they decided to teach him a lesson. A minor difference of opinion resulted in a full-blown war. Was it avoidable? Absolutely. So why did this guy respond so rudely? He knew that he was wrong. If he was in the queue and somebody else would have done this, he too would have objected. So then why didn't he smile, request others to let him go first, and respond politely? What made him forget these basic rules of interaction?

I can elaborate on countless number of instances where poorly chosen words worsen the situation. This is a very serious issue these days and must be dealt with. People venting anger on social media and social networking sites on issues which do not even directly concern them is very common. They even have a name now, 'Trolls'. As I started writing this book, three very interesting things happened in India. First, the Aam Aadmi Party (AAP) won 28 seats in the Delhi elections and were invited to form the government. Second, India's foreign diplomat to the US was arrested on an issue that involved a domestic servant and forged VISA documents. And third, the Supreme Court dismissed a petition seeking review of a judgement that upheld the criminalization of homosexuality in section 377 of Indian Penal Code. My Facebook, Twitter and Google social circle were abuzz with all these topics. I sometimes wondered—why would someone express so much anger on an issue that is not connected to them in any way. And I never figured out who their anger was directed towards or what were they angry about. One guy wrote on his wall, 'F*&^ America for its double standards'. And this guy works for a reputed American company. Why would he write this on his wall for the whole world to see? How would his colleagues, peers, seniors and juniors feel about this? He stayed in that country for over 5 years, made lot of money, and now comes back to write 'F*&^ America'. Why? What did he achieve by doing this? Did America change by his reaction? Did anybody change a bit? So why write something like this which has no connection to anyone except you? It is not so simple though. We enjoy freedom of speech, but sometimes things can go too far.

About the Book

Every day we find ourselves in some of the above mentioned situations. We are often asked to respond to difficult questions posed by people in their capacity as our bosses, members of the family, or friends. And in the spur of the moment, we have to think and respond as intelligently as possible, simultaneously demonstrating our capability and addressing the issue. I think the time taken to efficiently and effectively communicate is the most important factor. Research suggests that most of the time conflicts arise due to a faulty choice of words and the wrong tone used to utter them. (Colorado, 2005). Indian History is replete with number of examples to substantiate this point. Mahabharata being a repository of such examples. Ability to communicate well not only resolves conflicts but also makes life much pleasurable.

Importance of Conveying the Right Message

Here are few examples on how the right message can bring you success. Here's the first one. I heard this story from a senior colleague of mine when I newly joined the company. He said that he had heard it from someone senior to him who heard it from his senior and is sort of an urban legend within the company. This company was started somewhere in the late 80s by a group of cutting-edge scientists and PhDs. As the company grew and became profitable, they had to grow and scale their efforts. So they started recruiting. The problem was that they had never taken any interviews. Nevertheless they invited applications. When the shortlisted candidates came, they asked very tough scientific questions and rejected most applicants who answered incorrectly. One of the positions was HR Manager. A smart lady called Mary applied. And to her bad luck, the interview panel had one of the toughest nut in it—Bob. Bob was a maverick. A brilliant scientist, he had hundreds of patents to his name and while everyone respected him, he was not gifted with the best of social skills. So he would make very rude statements and turn people off. He hated this interview process, but knew that he had to help out the company. So Mary went to his room for her interview and saw Bob working on his computer. There was no greeting. Mary just sat down and waited. Bob asked, 'If you were to measure the efficiency of this logic that I have just developed, what are the best algorithms you would use'. Mary kept calm. She had a major in Human Resources and had done her undergrad in literature. She had no clue what the question meant. With a smile on her face she replied, 'I am not sure, but if you give me a moment, I will find out who can answer that for you.' Bob looked at her and said, 'You are hired'. Mary later became the VP of HR at this company. How did Mary think and say something so wonderful that Bob liked and got her the job? We all know that job interviews are very important. And having spent 12 years in the corporate world myself, I personally got tremendous opportunities in my career simply because I was able to communicate effectively to my interviewer.

Let's now take up another example which I learned at an entrepreneurship conference. There was a business idea contest few years ago hosted by an American university. The finals were organized in Berkeley. One of the participants (let's call him Samir) had a company which made artificial flowers. He took a bouquet of artificial roses with him in the flight cabin because they could have been damaged in his suitcase. When he landed in America, he was stopped by the customs who told him that any flowers, fruits, plants are prohibited and he has to leave behind his bouquet. Samir said that the flowers were artificial. The custom official did not believe him. He was taken to a room and an expert was called to investigate the flowers. After clearing the investigation, the entire custom department took a photo with Samir and his bouquet as a memory and let him go with good wishes. Samir took a taxi from the airport to his hotel and requested the driver to first take him to any flower shop. He wanted to take a look at the kind of flowers people bought there. His hotel was in the downtown and the taxi driver took him to one near his hotel. Samir walked inside with his bouquet and spent some time looking around. The owner of the shop asked him, 'Where did you buy these flowers.' Samir said, 'I make them.' The shopkeeper was amazed. He touched them, smelt them and immediately placed an order of USD100,000 for a consignment. Samir walked out of that shop with a signed contract and an advance check of USD10,000. The next day was his presentation for the finals and he hadn't even prepared. The next morning, he sat down in a room with many promising entrepreneurs like him. They gave amazing presentations to the judges and he got intimidated. Nevertheless, he thought that nothing can be done now and was more focused on his order that he had to fulfil. When his turn came, he presented his slides. There were just four. The first one had his name and his company information. The second slide had a photo of the entire US custom officials at the SFO airport with him and his flowers. The third slide had a copy of the USD10,000 check he had received last night from the florist and the last one was 'Thank you!'. Samir won the competition that year. As a teacher of managerial communication in B schools, I wish that my students make simple and effective presentations like this. Every day, more than 5 million presentations are being made or heard. What a colossal waste of time it would be if those presentations are boring and pointless. So these are few scenarios described above. One is a confrontation with palpable tension between both parties. The second is a job interview and the last is a corporate presentation (also called a pitch). I also mentioned different forms or modes of communication—one was verbal, the other was written, and the last was on an entirely new medium—the social network. The common thread between all scenarios is a subject called persuasive communication that I am very passionate about. As a doctoral student of persuasive communication, I spend a lot of time analysing words and speeches of famous leaders. Research suggests that one of the most important skill in a leader is to be able to persuade others to act. (Fluto, 1999) (Barrett, 2006) This is not just true for the corporate world. There are leaders in business, politics, entrepreneurship, academics, spirituality, humanities, and social arenas as well. Majority of them are excellent speakers and articulate communicators. Their followers are able to understand their views clearly and take action. The main purpose of this book is to help its readers be able to use persuasive communication in a variety of contexts they face—both at their workplace and outside.

Unfortunately, the subject of communication is not given the importance it deserves. I personally feel that the value of effective communication transcends corporate boardrooms and influences all sphere of our social lives. A lot of books have dealt with the theme of writing and presenting effectively in the corporate world. In my book, I intend to highlight the significance of communication as the most vital medium of human capability, be it day-to-day socializing, corporate presentations, giving/taking interviews, blogging, etc. I really hope this book makes the reader introspect and translate the contents of the book into concrete action.

I believe that efficient communication can help solve all problems of this world. It can be used to resolve conflicts at home or at the workplace, it can bring people together and set them on a larger goal that would help everyone and make this world a better place. The framework described in this book can be applied to any problem or situation that you may have that requires interaction with the other party. The book will have 'how-to' sections interspersed in the chapters to help the reader learn better.

CHAPTER 2

Why Communication Fails

12 MARCH, 1930, AN ORDINARY Indian challenged the might of the 150-year-old British Empire with the most powerful of weapons—words! Mahatma Gandhi inspired the masses and championed the arduous task of fighting the Colonial rule by travelling the length and breadth of the country and convincing people to unite in solidarity. Gandhi made a remarkable use of all forms of communication that could have been used to connect with the masses—speeches, newsletters, and one-on-one interactions. He conveyed the pre-decided day of 12 March for the Salt March, which triggered the wider Civil Disobedience Movement. The unthinkable happened when more than 10,000 followers walked alongside Gandhi to Dandi and broke the repressive salt law, braving the police. The followers had imbibed Gandhi's method of Satyagraha with such faith that despite brutal beating by the British police, they did not retaliate with violence. This event is of unprecedented importance in the history of the world because never before was a non-violent method of fighting the oppressor been used this effectively. It comes as no surprise then that Mahatma Gandhi occupies a place in most notable books on leadership.

On 16 June, 2013, Malala Yousoufzai had the world spellbound by her moving speech at the United Nations. She proclaimed herself as an ardent follower of Gandhi's philosophy of non-violence and brought the audience to tears with her story. The video of her speech went viral. (Youtube Malala, 2013). In 2014, Malala Yousafzai jointly received the Nobel Peace Prize with India's Kailash Satyarthi.

So how did Gandhi and Malala manage to influence people with their words? Are people born with the gift of the gab or is it an acquired skill? Did they prepare these talks or just woke up bright that morning, stood in front of the audiences, and rattled off words that came to them? Well, Malala had prepared as she was reading from a piece of paper. Maybe Gandhi too made notes before he addressed large gatherings. I will come back to this later in the book. But the point here is the effect Gandhi's words had on his listeners. They trusted him, liked him, and did what he told them to do. That is the simplest definition of leadership. He knew what to say, what not to say, and how to say it.

I strongly believe that effective communication is not a gift from above. It is a skill like any other that can be learned like cycling, swimming, parasailing, cooking, balancing accounts, creating strategic business plans, writing code, or making an android app. With the proper framework, which we discuss later in the book, training, practice, and most importantly— with a desire to learn—one can become a great speaker and, with time, a great leader too. The same approach can be applied to writing letters, emails, or internet blogs. To spread his message, Gandhi would write letters to his friends, fellow congress party workers, politicians, world leaders, governments, media, and would travel around the world making public speeches. He would call for prayer meetings and hold discourses on secularism. The content was simple without being too simplistic. He connected with his audiences by dressing like them and speaking like them. So it is no wonder that he became an inexhaustible reservoir of inspiration for so many.

So how did Gandhi create those messages? Can we also create simple and effective messages like him and persuade our audience? I believe that it is possible with time, patience, and practice.

Let's compare a leader making a brilliant speech to a chef making his star-dish. Let's say that this star-dish is a cake. There is a standard recipe to bake a cake. One needs flour, butter, and sugar as key ingredients. And the chef has to follow a series of steps to bake a good cake. But at the same time, the chef uses his own discretion to mix the ingredients as per his own choice and even gets a little creative with his technique of baking. It is also important for the chef to keep his customers in mind. If the chef works very hard and makes a really special black forest cake for a person who doesn't eat egg, or is allergic to berries and nuts, his entire effort is pointless. The person consuming the dish is paramount as the one who judges the taste and the merits and demerits. We usually love what we create. It is only the other person who has the potential to critically assess our creation, be it a painting, a book, or a dish. A good chef will never even start the baking process without a good understanding of the palate of those who will eat the cake. He will then choose the recipe accordingly.

Another example is the similarity between creating a message and DJing. A DJ has a lot of tools, instruments, and hi-tech devices to make his music. But a good DJ knows what will get his audience in a groove and which genre of music to play. However, it is the listener who judges whether the music makes the cut or not. If he doesn't like it, he will walk out of the club and go to one which offers better music.

Here is a Facebook update of a friend. He was in a conference and this is what he posted.

Was at some obscure tech-seminar yesterday. The speaker was a project-manager-turned-unit-head-because-he-finally-had-to-be-promoted-somewhere. Some gems:

Speaker: Lot of people are thinking what is cloud. Cloud is very simple, you are today wanting something, all you have to do is take this thing and within 10 mins you are having the thing.

Audience: But what about security?

Speaker: See today people are getting killed in ATMs. After so much security also all this is happening. So as long as there is human, they can be sold. Today he is working for Tata, tomorrow he will work for Accenture. So where is security? All this questions are rising only when the person is not of strong character.

I was very amused by this post. The speaker must be a very highly qualified engineer. His responses not only suffered from poor grammar, but also did not relate to the topic or the audience. Why does this happen? Why don't speakers realize this simple thing? They are all smart, well educated professionals. Communication through words is very basic and unique to human beings. It comes as simply as walking. Our parents taught us to walk and from then on, we do it without any problem. So how do we forget communicating effectively? It is an art that we already know; we just need to labour a little more to attain perfection. There are lot of good papers and research done on the barriers to communication. I recommend 'Barriers and gateways to communication', a paper written by Carl R. Rogers and F.J. Roethlisberger, both professors at University of Chicago and Harvard, respectively. (Rogers & Roethlisberger,

1991). But I will not get into the communication process which has a speaker, the medium and the listener as a collective entity. Instead, I will just focus on the barriers from a speaker's perspective only.

Reasons why a speaker fails to communicate effectively

1. Expecting that the audience also knows what we do

I chanced upon an interesting research explaining this phenomenon called 'the curse of knowledge' (Sunstrom, 2013). Here is what it said:

> In a famous psychological experiment, a group of subjects were divided into two: tappers and listeners. The tappers were asked to think of a song and try to rhythmically tap the song on a table, while the listeners were asked to listen and figure out which song the tappers were tapping along to. The tappers were 50 percent certain that the listeners would be able to identify the song they had had in mind while tapping, but the results of the experiment were shocking: only 2.5 percent of the listeners were able to figure out the song! In other words: the tappers overestimated their success ratio of being understood 20 times above how many times they actually were being understood. When we suffer from the curse of knowledge, we are like the tappers: just because we know the melody of the song we're tapping to, we inaccurately assume that others will know it too. But often, the other person—the listener—doesn't draw the same conclusions that we do because this person doesn't have the same information as

we do. In the case of the listeners, they weren't able to identify the tapping as a song, they only heard a series of discordant tappings. If we extrapolate these results to communication in general, it means that we think people understand what we're saying a hell of a lot more often than they actually do—because we're so used to knowing the things we know that we expect others to know it as well.

Does this imply that expertise or qualification hinder effective communication? Well, no. Knowledge is important and qualifications are a bonus as they demonstrate credibility of the speaker. I personally wouldn't trust a speaker who lacks sound knowledge and uses only rhetorical flourishes to persuade. So in my view 'the curse of knowledge' is nothing more than a blind spot in our knowledge that can be removed with little effort. Good leaders do not have this blind spot which is why their speeches are comprehended easily by their audiences. I will come to this point later on again.

2. Lack of preparation

Having spent 12 years in the corporate world, I must spill the beans—most of the presentations that I have seen are done with little or no preparation. I recall sitting in this important sales conference. The entire sales organization was out there and my colleague was supposed to give his update on the sales in his region, challenges, and recommendations. Usually these conferences happen in very jazzy locations like Las Vegas or some exotic island in some remote corner of the world. Everyone is jet lagged, tired and bored if not suffering from crushing hangovers from the previous night's drinking binge. It is common for a speaker who is scheduled to speak at 11 am, to start preparing at 10:30 am. They flick open their laptops, copy paste some slides from last year, brush up their numbers, add a few snazzy elements, and lo and behold! The presentation is ready. They spend no effort to practise the speech, don't even plan how to go about the topic. It is just a 'PPT session' with slides and the speaker is just accidental co-incidence in that room. This isn't limited to the corporate world; many conferences, events, seminars and talks have speakers who barely invest time to think and prepare a good talk. They think that confidence and good public speaking skills will suffice and they can figure out what to say when their turn comes. But I disagree completely. I have blundered myself as well. I was once invited to a top-notch conference as a panelist to represent my company. It was a golden opportunity for me to get noticed and establish myself in the industry. The who's who of the industry were present and I was humbled to be seated as a panelist with them. But I was not prepared. I just thought I would roll with the moment and wow my audiences. It was a disaster. I had no content on my slides, no notes for my speech, and made a complete fool of myself. All other speakers made very thoughtful presentations with data, examples, and sensible arguments which got good media attention as well. I was ignored completely. I felt bad, but I think I deserved it. Lack of preparation is a key cause for failing to communicate effectively with the audiences. Good leaders spend time thinking and preparing their messages. In a video on how presidential speeches are created, Jon Favreau, speechwriter for Barack Obama, mentions that Obama spends a lot of time preparing his speeches. He goes over the drafts personally and practices whenever he can. (Kennedy Forum Channel on Youtube, 2013)

3. Glossophobia

Glossophobia, or the fear of facing audiences, afflicts many, including me. It means getting tongue-tied due to the fear or anxiety of speaking. Here are some of the most commonly experienced symptoms of glossophobia

a. Blackouts
b. Cold fingers
c. Sweaty palms, foreheads
d. Dryness of mouth
e. Icy chill sensation down our back and spine
f. Blankness in the mind—fumbling for words
g. Increased heart beat
h. Wooziness
i. Paleness in the face
j. Frozen expressions and bodies

The audience sniffs all of this very easily and when they do, they switch off. The speaker has to really work hard to avoid letting the audience know about his weakness. The good news is that this can be overcome. It requires lot of hard work and patience though. And one can find lot of solutions to overcome glossophobia—from counselling experts to books to professional trainers galore. In fact, there is a website called glossophobia where one can find lot of resources to help them through.

4. Lack of creative thinking

If we reconsider the example I gave in Chapter 1 of our friend from a top IT MNC who explained the Cloud to the audience, it is clear that this person just did not seem to possess the skill to think creatively. He may have the requisite degrees, but he failed to effectively communicate his knowledge on the subject to his audience. Our brain is the key to a world of unknown possibilities. It is akin to a computer with millions of neurons that once fired properly can really propel us to higher intelligence. Imagine you buy a Harley Davidson bike with 2200bhp and limit its use to buying milk from the nearby grocery store that is 10 meters away and drying clothes after washing. What a waste, right? I think we are like that Harley Davidson bike. We have a lot of latent potential that needs to be utilized to its full capacity. Our education system still often follows the method of rote learning and that constricts out-of-the-box thinking. Awe-inspiring leaders carve their niche by thinking in an innovative manner. But what does it take to widen the horizons of the mind and think beyond the mundane and the usual? A simple trait—curiosity. The desire to know and explore the uncharted territories help keep the mind engaged and creatively stimulated. The more you learn, the more creative you get. For example, books are a great way to learn. In a simple experiment done by researchers, it was found that the brain of those who read books showed increased activity, which could lead in an increase in brainpower. This may also result in a greater creativity which could be helpful in making good messages. An ability to use words in imaginative ways always enhances the novelty factor of the message. (Ferro, 2014)

The endeavour to follow your heart's passion also fuels creativity. Artists are also great examples of personalities who communicate their ideas in unheard-of and imaginative fashion. David Lance Black, a famous screenwriter who has written scripts for Oscar-nominated movies talks about his creative process. He says that he spends at least a year in researching the topic and another year in the outline. Once that happens, he brings out a 'Vomit Draft' and then spends a good few months in polishing it till it is ready as a movie. The entire creative process is very lonely and laborious. But the output is an Oscar-nominated movie. (Black, 2014)

5. Know thy audience

I was called to give a lecture on career choices to the students of Kendriya Vidyala in Bangalore in 2003. I was working in Intel at that time. So, prepared for a session on 'careers in hardware', I entered the room. I was surprised to find many young children also sitting there. So I started my diatribe about Intel processors, RISC, CISC, North Bridge, South Bridge...and suddenly, a small piece of chalk landed on my foot. I ignored it and continued. After two minutes, a paper plane landed near my foot and I heard hushed giggles from the audience. There was a full-on chalk fight in progress with paper planes whooshing past. It did not take me long to realize that it was a chaos engineered by my talk. I had prepared a talk for an audience which was not ready for it. I let this go on for a couple minutes. My laptop was connected to a big sound system. I loaded a game called NASCAR and started playing. The students suddenly heard loud sounds of cars screeching on the race circuit and saw really cool graphics on the overhead screen. They were spellbound; chalks and planes forgotten. Then I took the mike and asked, 'Want to play?' 'Yes,' they screamed and made a beeline for me. I let them play for 5 minutes and then switched off the projector. There was a collective 'awwwwwww' from the children. 'Do you want to know how that game is made?' I asked them. 'YES'. So for the next 20 minutes, I talked about my work in graphics at Intel, how the games were made and how the young children could look at a career in playing computer games in the future. I learnt a big lesson that day—never misjudge your audience. Many speakers don't even bother to understand their audience. The curse of knowledge, as I mentioned above, plays a double whammy here. Many speakers make insensitive remarks which can also backfire on them if they are not aware of their audience. There has been a case of this at a conference in 2013. The speaker made a sexist remark which offended a lady in the audience. She tweeted about it. As the speaker spoke, the tweet went viral and caught international attention. The organizers of the conference were left red-faced and so were the companies that were participating. The next day, both the speaker who made that comment and the lady who tweeted about it got fired from their jobs. (Cutler, 2013). There is no greater sin for a leader than to say something that may hurt his audience.

Chapter 3

How Leaders Persuade: The AEIOU Xtra E Framework

A BRIEF HISTORY OF PERSUASION

The simple art of using words to get what you want done is called persuasion or influence. This definition is commonly used in the world of business and politics. However, it is also applicable throughout our lives in all scenarios that we may find ourselves in. It takes basic communication principles and a little common sense to get others to do what you want them to do. The earliest mention of persuasion was in the Vedic ages, in 1200 BC, where a good king was expected to possess certain knowledge and skills to run a kingdom efficiently. One of these skills was called Samvachya or Sanpathya or the art of conversation. (Bharadwaj, 2013). Later, in 300 BC, Chanakya, philosopher, scholar, and adviser to King Chandragupta Maurya, and author of *Arthashastra* and *Chanakya Neeti*, mentioned that one of the important skills for a king to be a good administrator was good communication skills (or Vangmi). Not unlike present day management gurus, Chanakya emphasizes the importance of knowledge, skills, and attitude. (Jain & Mukherji, 2009)

In 350 BC, Aristotle wrote *Rhetoric*—a comprehensive documentation on the communication model for leaders. The original work was in Latin which was later translated to English and other languages in early twentieth century by various scholars. (Kennedy, 1991)

However, from that period to the mid-nineteenth century, hardly anything of note was written on communication as a subject. In the late nineteenth and early twentieth century, there was some progress in addressing this topic by academics and researchers. One of the triggers for this progress were the World Wars and the need to understand communication as a tool to influence and persuade people to action.

Between 1960s and 80s, the business schools and the corporate world saw a greater need for this subject, which fueled its progress and further research. Henry Mintzberg was one of the first proponents of demystifying the role of a manager in an organization. His path-breaking study was published in 1973 in the book *What the Manager Actually Does*. His latest book, *Managing*, was published in 2011, building further upon the study of 1973. It highlights that on a typical day, a manager is spending his day mostly fire-fighting, attending meetings, getting interrupted, or getting trapped in situations where he has to find solutions to get work done. (Mintzberg, 1973). Till then, the myth was that a manager is supposed to be thinking and making plans for others to work on. But his study brought out the essential aspect of a manager as a key influencer in an organization. Communication skills have become a large component of this activity. Many researchers claim that a manager will spend 70-90 percent or more of his time communicating with various stakeholders to get his work done. (Eccles, et al., 1992). When CEOs and other senior executives in all industries and countries are asked to list the most important skills a manager must possess, the answer consistently and not too surprisingly, includes—good communication skills. (GMAC, 2014). Managers spend most of their day engaged in communication; with the advent of cell phones, e-mail, text messaging, social media, etc, if that same study were done today, the number would be even higher. The sheer amount of time managers spend communicating underscores how important strong communication skills can be for the manager desiring to advance to leadership positions; thus, mastering leadership communication should be a priority for managers who want their organizations or the broader business community to consider them as leaders. (Barrett, 2006)

A study was conducted by an academic called Frank Fluto on a simple question—Is there a connection between leadership and communication? (Fluto, 1999). He met several employees from various companies and conducted a survey on how they perceive their managers. The study suggests that communication competence is indeed a necessary prerequisite for effective leadership. Another study mentions that for an organization to be productive, its front line managers should become leaders, and communication is one of the most important strategic tools for them to be able to influence their teams positively. (Ahmed, et al., 2010). A group of researchers did a study to co-relate communication and leadership styles. The study revealed that charismatic and human-oriented leadership are mainly communicative, while task-oriented leadership is significantly less communicative. The communication styles are strongly and differentially related to knowledge sharing behaviours, perceived leader performance, satisfaction with the leader, and subordinate's commitment to the team. (Vries, et al., 2009). So overall, there seems to be enough literature and evidence pointing to a strong link between a leader and a need for good communication skills. And we can argue that to be a good leader, one must have strong communication skills to persuade others into action.

YOUR WORDS HAVE AN IMPACT ON YOUR AUDIENCE

As I was writing this book, political parties in India were readying for General Elections 2014. The country saw three political leaders of three different political parties take centrestage—Rahul Gandhi of the Congress, Narendra Modi of the BJP, and Arvind Kejriwal of the AAP. This was a contest unlike any other in recent years—whether it was the run-up to the elections or the results. Newspapers and TV channels were constantly quoting the politicians' words, analysing their styles of speaking, and predicting the equations of power based on their ability to persuade the voters. For the first time, the ability of a leader to speak well was being connected to the possibility of him becoming the future PM of India. As we've seen, the media hasn't been kind to former Prime Minister Manmohan Singh. He was often ridiculed on his inability to express himself. Many leaders took a dig at him christening him the 'silent PM'. This only demonstrates how demanding the audiences are and how critical it is to, not just act, but speak like a leader. About time for us to take this subject more seriously than we do today. It is no wonder that India elected Narendra Modi with a thumping majority. Even a common man on the street seemed to know him and chants of 'Abki baar, Modi sarkar' were heard, regardless of culture, religion, and language. It became a marching order for the troops and the results amply demonstrated the impact of these four words. There are very interesting analyses done by academicians on how these political leaders speak. A professor in IIT Delhi did an illuminating analysis on Narendra Modi that is worth reading. (Nair, 2013). This will give you an insight on the various ways the audience can perceive you.

Let us first look at the phenomenon that swept Delhi for a few months. Arvind Kejriwal founded the Aam Aadmi

Party, contested the state elections, won 28 seats and was invited to become the chief minister of Delhi. How did he and his party achieve this in such a short time? Nobody even knew about him till about three years ago until Anna Hazare became the crusader against corruption with Kejriwal as one of his lieutenants. He then branched off and started the Aam Aadmi Party. Kejriwal made his stand very clear to everyone as a common man of India fighting against corruption and also named the party 'Aam Aadmi Party' to lay stress on that stand. He chose a *jhaadu* as his party symbol. The easily recognizable symbol stood for sweeping away the dirt from the political system and making life of a common man better. But think once again—why was he able to become the CM (though only for 49 days) and not anybody else? I think it was a combination of his track record and the tactful use of words that built a momentum. When he spoke, people listened. I was watching one of his videos where he explained what he and his party want to do. Swaraj (democracy). (YoutubeKejriwal, 2013). Without sounding preachy, he took the word 'swaraj' and connected it to the travails of a common man in a small locality of Delhi. He maintained the Aam Aadmi philosophy throughout the speech and made it clear that democracy, ideally, should take into account the needs of the common man. With a simple story, he gave an example of how his party workers achieved this and finished the speech by re-emphasizing what he and his party will do for the common man.

Following are some of the thoughts that crossed my mind when I saw that video

- I could understand every word of this speech
- What he said made sense to me
- I related to the story and could even visualize myself in it

- I felt motivated after listening to the speech
- I might vote for this party

Good speakers plan this outcome from their audiences before they make their speech. They draw the audience in through their story, make them relate to it with examples, and make them experience the situation through their words. It's like an artist giving a performance to an audience The success of that performer is measured by the response of the audience. The same analogy applies to leadership. Success of a leader is palpable when there is somebody to follow him and do what has been asked of him.

'Be Beautiful Inside'—the Dynamics of a Speech

Lupita Nyong'o shot to worldwide fame for a variety of reasons. One of those was her bold performance that won her the Oscar in the movie *12 Years a Slave*. But there was a more important reason. She won the hearts of every person who has faced racism in some form or the other by her inspiring words. The day she won the Oscar, her speech called 'Essence Black Women in Hollywood' went viral on social media. The current views on that video as I write these words are above 3 lakh. And this is just one of the videos. There would be many more versions of the video and collectively, they would have reached millions of viewers throughout the world. So let me take this video and use it as an example of how the dynamics of a good speech work.

1. **The importance of understanding your audience:** Let's first see the perspective of the audience. They are the real reason why this speech has become popular. Without an audience, there can be no leader. And a good speaker

understands this dynamic very clearly. They know that the speech is their message 'FOR' an audience. Let me give you an example to make this easier to understand. Imagine that you invite your boss who has arrived from the US for dinner. You and your wife have taken great care to make your home look warm, comfortable, and welcoming. Lights and candles are lit. A variety of Indian dishes are prepared for the guest like palak paneer, bhelpuri, parathas, raita, salads, and gulaab jamuns. The boss comes home and as he sits on the table, he says, 'I forgot to tell you that I am vegan'. You and your wife smile and don't quite get what that means. You offer him palak paneer and he refuses because vegans do not eat any animal products. Paneer, or cottage cheese, is made from milk which comes from a cow (or a goat). You offer parathas which he again refuses as they are fried in ghee which comes from animals. You then realize that raita can't be offered either. You sheepishly ask him, 'Would you like to have some bhelpuri—it's an Indian snack'. Your boss says, 'Sure'. And you are relieved. The boss takes a spoonful and suddenly says, 'I am sorry I can't eat that. It has peanuts. And I am allergic to peanuts.' You are heartbroken and feel embarrassed. Your wife gives you an I-am-going-to-kill-him-and-bury-you look. The boss is very apologetic too and says, 'I am sorry, I should have informed you earlier. But I assumed that you spoke to my secretary and she would have informed you of all this.' You hadn't and are quite crestfallen. So that evening, your boss ate the salad which thankfully did not have any animal product in it. If you would have asked the boss about his dietary preferences in advance, this could've been avoided. Just as a chef makes food 'FOR' an audience, similarly, a speaker prepares his message

'FOR' the audience. Your overall message may remain the same, but you can change your words and tone to suit the audience. The audience can come from a variety of backgrounds and cultures and may have their own views on a topic. It's your job to understand, appreciate, and tune your message accordingly. The audience is also very easily distracted. Every 3 seconds, a text or a notification appears on their phone screens. They also may have biases against the topic or you as a speaker. Many times, they might not even know who you are and may have a persistent 'why should I care or listen to you' banging in their heads as you are speaking. And most importantly, they want to know the answer to 'What do you want from me' as quickly as possible. A good speaker asks the following questions to understand his audiences

a. What is the background of my audiences (age, culture, sex, location, educational qualification, work experience etc)
b. What are their belief systems, values, likes, and dislikes
c. What are their views on the topic I am speaking about
d. What would they like to know from me
e. What can I offer them
f. What do I want them to do at the end of my speech (message)

2. **The importance of preparation**: Lupita read from a piece of paper. I am pretty sure that she didn't write that speech the night before the Academy Awards. I think a lot of preparation went into it, though she categorically denied it in the opening lines. Coming from a prestigious school

(Lupita went to the Yale School of Drama) also provides a sound foundation and exposure, and years of practice do come in handy at times like these. This is the second important dynamic of a good speaker—they prepare and practise. Some of the world's best leaders still practise meticulously before they speak in front of an audience. Churchill was often heard practicing in the bathroom and Obama would revise and re-revise the speech transcript many times over before an event. Let me explain what I mean by preparation by the 10,000-hour rule as an example. (Gladwell, 2009). It takes hours and hours of practice for a pilot to get certification for flying a passenger aircraft. The whole idea of this practice is to help the pilot master the craft of flying a plane, take decisions in split seconds, and perform his job better at that moment when he is flying that plane. The adage 'practice makes perfect' applies to speaking as well. There is ample research to demonstrate that if a person goes through a step-by-step method of doing something, learning is faster and, very soon, it becomes a behaviour. Think of the first time you tried to ride a bicycle. Our parents or elders taught us how to balance ourselves on the bicycle; we fell a few times but learnt how to pedal and balance together. With time, we could cycle with ease and now it comes almost naturally to us. A pilot also has a similar experience. With time, and by repeated practice sessions in the flight simulator, he learns to fly a mega-ton jumbo jet. Nelson's legendary words after he defeated Napoleon were, 'The battle of Waterloo was won in the fields of Eden.' He meant that before he and his army entered the Waterloo battlefields, they did a lot of practice in the fields of Eden. These practice sessions helped them perform better on that day.

Preparation readies our mind and our body to do a task better. NASA trains its astronauts for years before they can even qualify for a space flight. I always wondered why it would take so many years of preparation for sitting in a sealed rocket and going on a space flight. The answer was given by my childhood icon, Wing Commander Rakesh Sharma, in a talk that I attended. He said that the human brain is trained to walk on earth because of how it perceives gravity through our legs. But in space, or on the moon, there is no gravity and hence no feedback of movement. So the brain has no way to understand how to walk or move. And that is the training they go through. Without that training, it will be impossible for astronauts to move or do anything. And if you have seen the Oscar-winning movie *Gravity*, you will realize how difficult it is to manage one's body in space. A simple push can send you reeling and if you are not trained to handle such a situation, you might not survive. Sumo wrestlers in Japan go through intense years of preparations including diet plans and a complete shift in lifestyle to perform like a sumo wrestler someday. Ask any performer—a dancer, a singer, an instrument player, an acrobat, or anyone who has to perform in front of a large audience. I bet you that they spend hours and hours practising their craft before they go on stage. So why don't we all consider ourselves as performers too? Our craft is that of conveying a message and making our audience act in a certain way. Churchill once said, 'If I have to speak for 5 minutes, I need a week of preparation. But if you want me to speak for 1 hour, I am ready now.' This means that shorter the performance, longer is the time investment required to prepare and perform. A good thumb rule that I follow is 10-10-10. I start preparing at least 10 days before my event, do at least 10 revisions of my speech, and speak at least 10 times in front of the mirror for my practice. I sometimes also record myself using the webcam and review myself. It works wonders. In my earlier days, I used to ask my wife to sit through and evaluate my speeches critically. Your spouse would be a great critic for your practice sessions.

3. **The importance of a style**: Lupita wore an expensive designer gown that made her look elegant. She stood straight, smiled, and sometimes even broke down as she spoke. On the day of the Academy Awards, she wore a tiara and looked every bit a princess. Her blue flowing gown was the talk of the media. She was stylish and the world took notice. Taking my argument that I made in the last section, that a speaker is like an artist performing in front of an audience a little further, each performer has his own natural or acquired style of speaking and conveying a message. If I were to look at some of the TED talks—which are a great repository for all of us to watch and learn from—many of the speakers demonstrate the following styles

   a. They all are confident and comfortable—or at least they seem to be. They might be quite nervous inside but as a viewer of that talk, I find them confident. Confidence is demonstrated in the way they stand, talk, and conduct themselves.
   b. They are heard clearly—voice (tone, pitch, modulation) is a very important element of one's style. You need not worry about pronunciation if you have a clear voice that can be heard and understood by everyone.

c. They look into the eyes of the audience and the camera—every member in the audience loves it when a speaker looks straight at them. That's the best way to connect and appreciate your audience.
d. The face, body, and hands are very well coordinated with the words. They change facial expressions according to the message, use hands to explain a concept better, and use their body postures to convey confidence. Some move around, some stand rooted to the same place. Some use their hands like Zubin Mehta and some do not. Some smile and convey a range of meaning through their faces and some have no expressions at all.
e. Dressing style and presence—Remember the quote 'first impression is the last impression'. Sadly, it's true and plays a vital role in front of audiences. The way we dress and look pretty much decides our impressions on the audiences. They have every right to judge us and we cannot control it. Good speakers and leaders plan their appearance very well. The pose, the smile, and the colours—everything is coordinated and planned for maximum impact on their audiences.

4. **The right words and crafting the message**: How did Lupita choose those beautiful words that became such a sensation? Now, I confess, I don't have the answer on how Lupita did it. I don't know her from Adam. But after spending a few years poring over various speeches like this, I can definitely say that there is a method to writing these words. And this is what I will focus on from now no in this book. Lupita began by telling the audience that she will read out a letter she received from

a young girl. She read out lines from that letter as a story to her audience. She mentioned how that little girl, who felt she was not beautiful because of her skin colour, felt inspired by Lupita. She then connected that with her own childhood where she felt that her dark skin was a curse from God and how she prayed every night to God to make it whiter so she could feel beautiful. She then highlighted how detrimental it could be for a young girl to not feel beautiful and how a person's skin colour plays a role in that. She chose very careful words that conveyed a cry from her heart and drew the audience in. She then inspired them with a strong message to feel 'beautiful inside'. I am sure that many viewers could have related to this speech because we are conditioned to think that white is beautiful. FMCG companies who sell 'whitening' creams use this trump card a lot. In India, we have bigger problems. In arranged marriages, the groom's family desires a 'fair' girl and girls with dark complexions may not find good suitors. The western world too is far from tolerant when it comes to racial issues. But Lupita stayed away from the controversy of black v/s white. She chose to say only those words that were measured on her own definition of beauty and steered the speech towards an inspirational message for everyone who felt like her. The event was for Black Women in Hollywood and the audience lapped up every word. (Essence, 2014). As she spoke, the audience nodded along, smiled, and cried. The next day, it was all over the social media. I called a couple of my friends who had posted this message and asked them what they liked about the speech. Here are some of the things they said

a. They felt Lupita spoke from the heart and was sincere.
b. Since she was black, they felt that the topic was appropriate for her to speak on. Her Oscar award also helped to make her credibility stand out.
c. They felt connected to her story because they feel similarly about the topic of fairness as a parameter of judging beauty.
d. They cried or felt moved by her words.
e. At the end of the speech, they felt elated and believed that to feel beautiful, one doesn't really need to be fair-skinned. It endorsed their own view and re-affirmed their definition of beauty.
f. Throughout the speech, they felt as if Lupita was speaking directly to them.
g. There was a clear objective that they understood very early. The entire speech and the examples she gave related to this objective.
h. They were never distracted by anything else as they watched this video. One of my friends also said that she heard nothing else except the speech, and then afterwards saw a couple of calls that she missed while watching.

In the last couple of years, I have studied how great leaders speak and have realized that their speeches have a pattern. Leaving aside the delivery style and focusing just on the message, the words, and the flow—a clear framework can be identified in these messages. All these speeches demonstrate one or more of the following six elements.

i. Attention: words, actions, or sentences that capture the attention of the audience
ii. Examples or logic: stories, data, anecdotes, examples, proof, and arguments to help the audiences accept the point of view
iii. I-factor/credibility of the speaker: to demonstrate authority or power over the topic, or to create an identity
iv. Objective of the message: a clear idea or central theme, or a specific, measurable action for the audiences
v. U-factor/connect with the audiences: establishing common ground with the audience
vi Emotional appeal: ability of the speaker to convey emotions inspire feelings

Here is a table of some of the sentences from Lupita 's speech where these elements come out.

Attention	I received a letter from a girl and I'd like to share just a small part of it with you. (Also her presence, her smile, how she seems to look at you.)
Examples/ Logic	And then Alek Wek came on the scene. A celebrated model, she was as dark as night… She was on all of the runways and in every magazine and everyone was talking about how beautiful she was. Even Oprah called her beautiful and that made it a fact.
I-factor/ Credibility	I remember a time when I too felt unbeautiful. I got teased and taunted about by night-shaded skin.

Objective	I want to take this opportunity and talk about beauty. Black Beauty. Dark Beauty… And so I hope that my presence on your screens and in the magazines may lead you, young girl, on a similar journey. That you will feel the validation of your external beauty but also get to the deeper business of being beautiful inside. There is no shade in that beauty.
U-factor/ Connect	I am surrounded by people who have inspired me, women in particular whose presence on screen made me feel a little more seen and heard and understood.
Emotion	My heart bled when I read those words… And every day I experienced the same disappointment of being just as dark as I had been the day before.

Read the sentences above carefully and then watch the video or read the transcript again. (Essence, 2014). You will note various other sentences that you can slot in the six buckets above. You will then see the beauty of this speech, how every word connects to the objective of the speech. The story telling style captures the attention of the audience. Lupita gives her own examples and establishes her authority as a black woman dealing with self-doubt. She gives examples of Alek Wek and Oprah. She connects with the audience by telling them how they inspired her and thanked them. And lastly, she takes her audience through an emotional roller-coaster. When I watched this speech, I first felt happy, then sad, then sadder still, and, finally, happy again. Once the speech ended, I felt inspired and motivated.

You can do this analysis on any speech and see how it fits in the boxes above. In the next few chapters, I will go through each of these six parameters in a little more detail and explain through an example of a great speech or speaker who uses that parameter well.

Before we move on, I want to simplify this six parameter framework so that we can remember it easily. Let's list them down first

i. **A**ttention
ii. **E**xamples
iii. **I-factor** or Credibility
iv. **O**bjective
v. **U-factor** or Connect
vi. **Xtra E**motional appeal

> This becomes simpler to remember—the AEIOU Xtra E framework.

Just like we need vowels to make a word, similarly, this framework helps us create our messages.

PART 2

Chapter 4

The Fundamental Laws of Communication

Human species, for all its specificities and individualities, is bound together by certain fundamental traits almost universal in nature. It is surely complex to understand, but nobody branded it to be an impossible task. Here we get to the heart of the book. But even for that we need to build our premise first. So let's proceed gradually towards our goal.

Rule number 1: The audience decides the success of the message

This may come as a surprise, but this is one of the foremost principles of effective public speaking. It takes a while to digest this part. You might flaunt your enviable degrees from top schools or be the senior most person in a firm but the moment you are giving a talk, presentation or even trying to convince your clients, you inevitably subject yourself to their judgement. So if you strongly believe in the famous Amitabh Bacchan dialogue from the movies—*Main apni kismet khud likhta hoon* (I write my own destiny), this is the time to question that belief. You don't really write your destiny. Your audiences do—especially in the world of business. Communication, by definition, is a two-party process with a medium in between. As senders of the message, we sometimes work very hard on our content and on choosing the right medium. But we forget the importance of the receiver of our message and the fact that they, after all, are why we created the message in the first place. We don't realize that if at the moment any the intended person refuses to listen to us, our message fails. As do we. The same law applies to the world of marketing. If you don't understand your customer and undermine the fact that the success of your product is decided by the ability of the customer to buy, you are history. Communication is a very critical component in marketing and is one of the 4 Ps of marketing, as defined by Prof Philip Kotler, called Promotions. (Kotler, 1967). A company creates its advertisements as messages for their customers. If the customers don't like the message, the product won't sell. And somebody will lose their job in that company. Remember the famous Motorola cell-satellite phone which was launched in the 90s? It was called Iridium. The world's best scientists and professionals from business created this engineering marvel that would truly disrupt the way we communicated with each other. The company studied the customer needs and blew billions of dollars to get this baby in the market. It failed. Customers had moved on to newer technologies and didn't need to carry a 3 kilo brick around which did not work inside offices. (Iridium, 2010). Clearly, the audiences decided the future of this product and the company.

UPA and Congress were demolished in the General Elections 2014. The people decided their fates. So don't forget the importance of your audiences. Study and analyse your audience, even before you attempt to prepare your message. Know them better and make sure you use this knowledge to prepare the message. If you don't know your audiences well enough, take help from those who do. For example, if you're making a presentation to a completely new company, you can find someone in your networks who knows them. Call them and ask them about this group. Make sure you have the answers to the following questions.

1. Who is my audience?
2. Use the Kotler model of segmentation of your audiences as below (Philip Kotler, 2013)

    a. Demographic information: age, gender, income group, ethnicity, religion, educational qualifications, position in the company, etc
    b. Behavioural information: attitudes towards a product, beliefs, etc
    c. Psychographic: lifestyle habits, what they read, eat, etc
    d. Geographic: where are they from, what languages they speak
    e. Miscellaneous: any other information you can gather. An important data point for you can be their LinkedIn profiles, Facebook, Twitter, WhatsApp, etc..Basically any relevant information that you can obtain without resorting to illegal methods. Of course, my idea is not to promote stalker-like or voyeuristic tendencies!

3. **What are their expectations from you**: remember that your audience is a person, or people, similar to you. So when you put yourself in their shoes, you will realize how they want the same things that you would want as a member of the audience. Fundamentally, from a communication perspective, they want you to respect their time, be brief and come straight to the point without beating around the bush. Here are few things they ask from you as a speaker.

a. Who are you
b. What do you want from me
c. Why should I agree with you/Prove your point (Convince me)
d. What's in it for me
e. How do I act on the things you are asking me to do

Once you get a better understanding about the composition of your audience and their expectations from you, it will be a lot easier for you to prepare a message that caters to their needs. Communication is like cooking food. If you don't know your audience, it could be a disaster. It is like being a top chef who is renowned for the most delicious dark chocolate cake in the world—dribbling with chocolate, so soft that it melts in the mouth. But to me, that cake may be totally unappetizing as it contains egg and I am a vegetarian. So if the chef ignores that, he is the worst chef for me. I really don't care for his fame or his ability to please others. His cake does not work for me. Period. The sooner you realize the significance of this, the more efficient you will be in persuading your audience. In so many ways, communication is like a Shakespearean drama performed in front of an audience and it involves dancing and singing to their tune for approval and applause.

I am often asked about the ethical concerns associated with pleasing the audience and dancing to their tune by my students. This is obviously a loaded question and I would like to break it into two parts. I ask my students, 'Do you want to get things done or not?' the response is mostly affirmative. 'In that case,' I tell them, 'you must do whatever you need to for your audiences, which is within boundaries. If you feel what you are doing is unethical, then don't do it. Change your job.' This is a choice we have. So go ahead and exercise your choice. I have never felt that I am doing anything unethical in my classes. In fact, I *am* dancing in front of my students all the time. I have to engage them, entertain them, and make sure they learn. So it's my job to understand their needs and cater to them. If I come with boring slides, rattle off some words and walk away, it would not make a very useful class, will it?

Many times, we tend to overthink things. The writing is very clear on the wall. Audiences matter! Now if you are not comfortable with it, you are welcome to find a job where you will never meet customers, never meet your teams, never meet your boss, and generally manage to be an island unto yourself.

Rule number 2—Actions are louder than words

Albert Mehrabian, a professor at UCLA did pioneering work in the field of non-verbal communication. (Mehrabian, 1972). His studies are often misquoted by the application of mathematics in the world of communication skills training. Many self-proclaimed trainers use his 7:38:55 rule and which says 'only 7 percent of all communication happens in words. The rest—93 percent—happens through non-verbal communication aspects which include the tone of the voice (38 percent) and the rest 55 includes gestures, facial expressions, posture, etc. Well, in many ways this argument does hold well in the training programs. However, it falls flat when we consider written communications like emails, social media, and telecons, etc, which are a big bulk of today's corporate communication. (Straker, 2010). Let's see how this study impacts us in our lives by a simple example. Raj has had a hard day at work. His boss shouted at him. His deal didn't go through and it was just one of those terrible days. He is exhausted after a long painful drive back home, braving the traffic of Bangalore. He parks his car and rings the bell. The door opens and his little girl runs and jumps into his arms. He hugs her tight. She looks at him and says, 'What happened papa? You are not happy to see me?' Raj is taken aback. How did this little girl know that he was upset? Well, it's no rocket science. Your face gives away the answer. Raj looked tired. He didn't smile as much as he usually would. And a 3-year-old could understand. When we were kids, our mothers could catch us at lying by simply looking at our faces. The cold stare of our fathers when we broke something in the house was enough to terrify. Now imagine yourself making a presentation in front of your team. Even a mild sense of nervousness can be conveyed through your body language. That is why it is so important to smile and demonstrate positive body language.

The same example can be extended to all that we see or do. We all have experienced fights and conflicts within our families, with our friends, or with business partners. Usually, it emerges that the root cause of the fight was just the wrong tone of voice. The moment someone raises their voice or tone, it is a recipe for disaster. Even at the risk of sounding clichéd, I would like to reiterate the significance of a simple smile and a sincere 'sorry'. Remember the second law. Non-verbal communication is very important too. You cannot—and I cannot stress this enough—become a leader if you are not conscious of your non-verbal style as well. There are many cases where a very innocuous non-verbal gesture can result in catastrophe. One of my neighbours is a very grumpy old man. Someone parked their car in his slot and when he returned, he started honking and was visibly irritated. The person who had parked his car came back, and started apologizing profusely. My neighbor was standing with his hands on his hips and an angry expression on his face. He raised his voice and said, 'What right do you have to park your car here?' And that did it. The person didn't like his tone and his angry expression. He said, 'I said I am sorry. I had just parked for 5 minutes. And this is a public road. You really don't have a right to claim that it is yours.' The verbal dual began and both sides were at each other's throats. All this could have been avoided if they kept their tone pleasant and a scowl away from their face.

Here are some of the important elements of non-verbal communication that your audience tends to observe

1. Your smile
2. Your eye contact
3. Your facial expressions
4. Your handshake and mannerisms
5. Your posture—how you stand, sit, walk etc
6. Your gestures and hand movements
7. Your voice modulation, tone, pitch, the way you speak
8. Your appearance—how you look and groom yourself
9. Your dress—what you wear, what you project to others

Great leaders are conscious and in tune with non-verbal communication. They take immense care to know how they are seen by others and are constantly looking to learn. Again, as in a Shakespearean drama, an actor's non-verbal communication will add to the performance. Here's another one of my favourite examples. Barack Obama demonstrated ample non-verbal communication in the public address he made on the unfortunate Connecticut shooting spree in December 2012. He cried on national TV. Well, not cried as in bawled or any of the melodrama we see in our saas-bahu serials; but he choked up. He paused and wiped a tear from his eye very gracefully as he expressed his condolences to the families of those who died that morning. There was a moment of vulnerability that he showed through that gesture. But then, he hardened his face and displayed strength and valour. His tone became stronger as he uttered words to assure the audiences that action will be taken. (Obama, 2012). If you watch this clip and press the mute button, you can pin point the different gestures that Obama uses to communicate. They convey so much meaning that you don't need to listen to the words at all.

Rule number 3: Shut up and listen!

The first two laws are slightly easier to understand and assimilate in our behaviour. But the third rule is tougher to follow. Many of us who are married would be aware of the power of shutting up. Many successful marriages are built upon this law. It's called the law of listening. Actually, many marriages fail and fights erupt because they all ignore this law. In communication, there are two parties and a medium that connects them. A good leader knows when NOT to speak and when to listen. This word 'LISTEN' is actually made of the same letters as the word 'SILENT'. Both are very powerful methods used by leaders with their audiences. Dale Carnegie, in his bestselling book *How to Win Friends and Influence People,* dedicated a whole chapter on the art of being a good listener. If I ask you who your best friend is, chances are it will be a person who listens to you the most. That is the reason you love them so much. And it's not easy to find such a friend. It is almost as if we are driven by an innate need to speak continuously. We feel powerful when we say something to others. And in truth, it is very easy to speak. It requires very little effort to just shoot something from our mouths. On the other hand, listening requires us to spend more energy as compared to speaking. A wise man once said, 'Arrows, bullets and words are dangerous. Once released, they will always hit somewhere and leave a permanent scar.' Shooting bullets and words is easy. But restraining them is so darn hard.

Listening is a three-step process.

1. Shut up and absorb the information: Listen to what is being said. Quiet your mind, shut your mouth, and just allow your ears to take in the information. Stop processing immediately and, for heaven's sake, DO NOT open your mouth.
2. Demonstrate that you are listening: There is no worse insult to a person than to ignore them while they are speaking. This is very common in the corporate world. You are talking passionately to your boss about your idea and he is looking at his watch or his cell phone. Don't you feel insulted? Make proper eye contact. Lean towards your speaker and demonstrate that you are interested in hearing what they have to say.
3. Paraphrase what was said: This is the toughest part. Once the speaker has finished speaking, paraphrase what you understood in your own words. That way you can be sure that you heard right and the speaker also appreciates your listening abilities.

On phones, or in meetings, the moment someone starts speaking, our mind races to produce an answer. And if we don't restrain ourselves, we actually start responding. Many times, we start responding even before the speaker has finished speaking to us. This results in cross-talk or noise which is unproductive to both sides. The diagram below demonstrates good communication when we listen properly v/s bad communication.

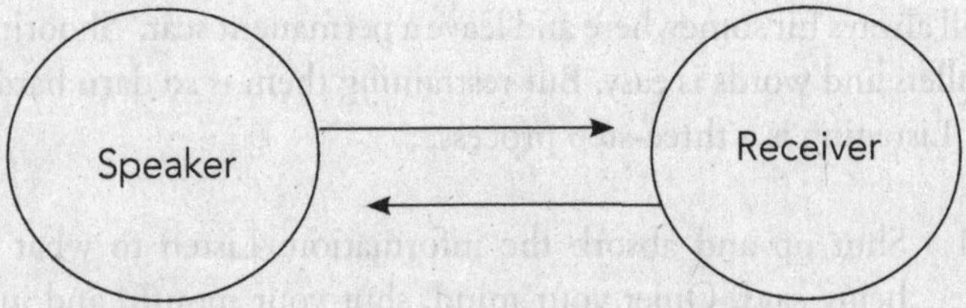

Noise because the receiver started to respond simultaneously and didn't listen fully.

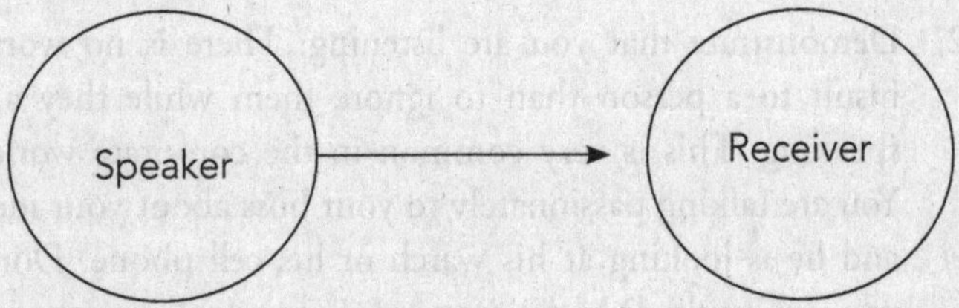

Speaker speaks. Receiver listens

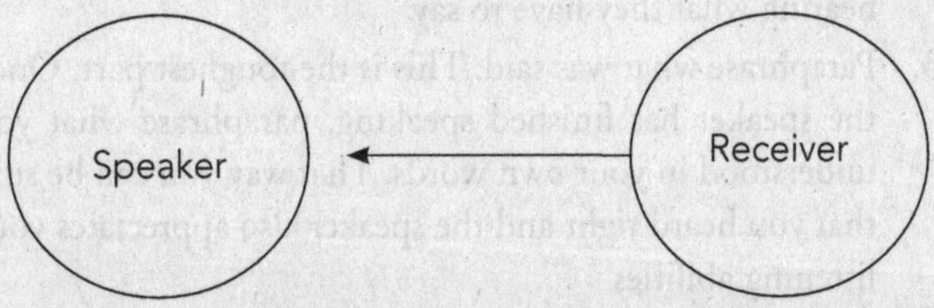

The roles reverse. The speaker now listens to what his receiver responds.

Listening is an art. It takes a lot of effort and practice to become a good listener. But once you start listening, your leadership curve will grow exponentially. The key is to understand and know when to apply this art. Here are some scenarios where you can shut up and listen.

1. In a conflict when tempers rise.
2. In a grievance when somebody is just venting out their views. You are not supposed to solve anything. Just lend them an ear; that may be all they need.
3. With your spouses, especially if you made a mistake which is the case most of the time. Even if you are right, just hear them out.
4. With your teams, especially your juniors when they come up with ideas.
5. With your customers, when they are giving you feedback.
6. In a meeting when somebody is asking a question or presenting a point of view.
7. In a telephone call when your voice is the only tool you have. So unless you hear the other party carefully, the conversation will be unproductive.
8. In a party when you don't know anybody. Use this art to enjoy the evening. Just walk up to someone, introduce yourself and once they say 'I am working in this company', let them do the talking. You can grab another martini, sit back and enjoy. But be honest to this process. Don't just lend them an ear. Lend them a *listening* ear using the three-step process mentioned above.

Exercises

1. You are a senior manager in a company. One of your team members, a girl called Asha, wants to meet you and has mentioned in an email that she wants to discuss something personal. She doesn't state the exact agenda and is disturbed. Which law would you apply in this situation to communicate and why?
2. You are a busy manager and have had a hard day at work. You have two small kids and they want you to take them to a movie. You are very tired. When you reach home, the kids are excited and ready to go for the movie. Your wife sees that you are not keeping well. She gets you a glass of water and says, 'You rest. I will take the kids out for the movie.' Which law of communication did the wife use and what was the impact?
3. You are participating in a debate in a college function. The topic given to your team is 'Should alcohol be banned in Kerala' and you are speaking against the motion. Which law of communication will apply for you to win the competition?

CHAPTER 5

The Objective

CREATING A PERSUASIVE MESSAGE IS a step-by-step activity. It requires us to understand and then apply the first law which I discussed in Chapter 4—The audience decides the success of the message. A critical aspect of this law is the need for the audience to ask the following questions to you as a speaker of the message.

1. What do you want from me
2. Who are you
3. Why should I agree with you/Prove your point (Convince me)
4. What's in it for me
5. How do I act on the things you are asking me to do

As a speaker, you must try to respond to all the questions above to make your message come across in the best manner. In this chapter we will discuss how to address the first question 'What do you want from me'.

Let's jump into role-play and simulate some common scenarios where you can apply the AEIOU Xtra E framework which we devised in Chapter 3. Imagine you are Ajay, a young MBA working in a big corporation that makes FMCG products for everyday use. The culture of the company is very open and you are quite new as compared to the veterans who work there.

You have been given a job to provide interesting analysis of the huge data that comes from all departments to the CEO's staff. There is a monthly meeting where you have to present a recent trend report to the staff two weeks from now. You are given five minutes to present in that staff meeting.

Let me ask you—what is the objective of your presentation? Here are some choices that I can provide you to choose from

1. To give an update to the staff on the various data models analysed
2. To show three slides and speak for 5 minutes
3. To impress the staff with your analytical and articulation skills
4. To give them certain points that leave an impression
5. To make them feel good and make their 5 minutes worthwhile
6. To have a good time and enjoy the presentation
7. To engage and interact with the staff, answer their questions satisfactorily
8. To have simple slides—more visual than textual

I did a similar exercise in a focus group that consisted of managers who work in the corporate sector. Most of them chose 1 and 4. I then went on to add another option number 9—All of the above. And it opened a can of worms. Some argued that if there are seniors and the CEO sitting in that room, one has to be very formal and serious. One person said that if we appear too flamboyant then it could spell doom for one's career. The seniors may think we are overconfident and full of fluff. One made a very interesting statement, 'They already know everything in the business. So telling them what they know already is a waste and I don't agree with point 4. I will probably focus on just point 1 because it's my job and get done with it.' Points 3, 5, 6 and 8 were vehemently opposed by many of them. A lady said, 'If I make slides with no heavy-duty charts and text, they may feel that I am incompetent.'

I did another exercise with another focus group. I asked them, 'If you are the CEO of a company and have a young MBA presenting data from different departments in your staff meeting for five minutes, what would you expect from him/her?' The answers were surprising. Here they are

1. I want to get 2-3 key points that I can use in my business operations
2. I don't want to see slides that have charts and numbers which I don't understand. These MBAs are too much into heavy slides that convey no meaning
3. I expect this person to know how to analyse data and articulate the problem in a way that I can understand
4. I want him to answer my questions satisfactorily. If he is not able to do so in that meeting due to lack of time or information, then at least he should be able to understand the questions and help in getting the answer later
5. I want to see an energetic, passionate young person who likes their job and is able to convey this by the way they present. Most of these presentations are so boring
6. I am giving them five minutes of my time. I hope they realize that their talk better be worth my time

This is a strange phenomenon in the corporate sector. As an audience, one expects a lot from their presenters but when they have to present themselves, they don't want to do what the audience expects them to. And it doesn't take a genius to figure out that the majority of presentations in the corporate sector are a complete waste of time, simply because the biases are very high. As I mentioned earlier, this is one of the reasons why communication fails. And the answers above are the proof.

If you want to become an effective leader, then start working on how you interact with your audience. In the previous Chapter, I had mentioned three laws of communication. The first law states that the audience decides the success of the message. So if you are to make a presentation for your CEO's staff for five minutes, you better start doing what they expect from you. Or else, your presentation will be one of those boring presentations which nobody would attend if it were not compulsory. These five minutes are your chance to get noticed and potentially transform your career. Don't you want your CEO to take notice of your work, use your key messages in his presentations, and treat you as a capable manager? If yes, then why do you not take this topic seriously?

Let's go back to our problem statement—if you are to present for five minutes to your CEO, you should make all eight points mentioned above your objectives. Yes, it is hard to achieve all of them in five minutes, but it is not impossible. Start with asking yourself, 'What is the purpose of my presentation?' In simple words, what do you want your audience to do or feel at the end of the five minutes? The purpose of the presentation is the most important bit for you because it will guide you and help you articulate yourself better.

On 12 July, 2013, a young girl from Pakistan shook the world with her words. She spoke for a mere fifteen minutes at the United Nations in front of leaders from around the world. Here are some sentences from Malala Yousafzai's speech that outline her purpose. (Yousuf, 2013)

> So here I stand, one girl among many. I speak not for myself, but for those without a voice. Those who have

fought for their rights. Their right to live in peace. Their right to be treated with dignity. Their right to equality of opportunity. Their right to be educated.

I am here to speak for the right of education for every child. I want education for the sons and daughters of the Taliban and all the terrorists and extremists.

So today, we call upon the world leaders to change their strategic policies in favor of peace and prosperity. We call upon the world leaders that all of these deals must protect women and children's rights. A deal that goes against the rights of women is unacceptable.

We call upon all governments to ensure free, compulsory education all over the world for every child. We call upon all the governments to fight against terrorism and violence. To protect children from brutality and harm. We call upon the developed nations to support the expansion of education opportunities for girls in the developing world. We call upon all communities to be tolerant, to reject prejudice based on caste, creed, sect, color, religion or agenda to ensure freedom and equality for women so they can flourish. We cannot all succeed when half of us are held back. We call upon our sisters around the world to be brave, to embrace the strength within themselves and realize their full potential.

So let us wage a glorious struggle against illiteracy, poverty and terrorism, let us pick up our books and our pens, they are over most powerful weapons. One child, one teacher, one book, and one pen can change the world. Education is the only solution. Education first.

Her speech was roughly 1500 words and the objective or purpose of the speech that is reproduced above is 300 odd words. That is twenty percent of the speech. The objective was clear, specific, and demonstrated her intent to her audiences around the world. A lot has been written about this speech and it has been analysed threadbare. But I want to just focus on the objective bit of it right now. A purpose is extremely critical in a message regardless of whether it is an email, a presentation, or a phone call to your customer.

A brilliant example of clarity and precision of objectives is from Mahatma Gandhi's famous Quit India speech. Imagine that you are Bapu and you have to convey a message to an entire country in an era where there was no technology. The only way was to either physically meet people or give out pamphlets that were printed in a printing press. Two simple words emerged from that speech—Quit India. And these became a chant for the Indians. His other speeches on the Swadeshi Movement had an equally simple and impactful objective. He asked his audience to avoid wearing clothes that were not made in India, boycott products that were not manufactured in India and retaliate if provoked. He himself demonstrated each of these objectives by wearing Khadi and practising ahimsa even when he was brutally beaten up and locked in jail. Malala quoted Gandhi in her speech as well.

Clarity of objective in a message puts everything else in perspective and makes it easier for you to create your message and your audiences to absorb it. The 2014 elections witnessed a leader making his objective very clear to the masses. 'Abki baar, Modi sarkaar' was on everyone's lips regardless of whether one liked him or not. The objective was stated in those four words. Now whether these four words were strung together by an adman is a completely different discussion altogether, the point holds. A clear objective is the starting point of a good message. In many ways, the art of drafting a message is like an architect thinking about creating a structure. He starts with an objective or a purpose of that structure. If the structure is used as a gas station, he will then apply different design aspects than those for a home. So before even jumping into creating the drawings of your rooms, think about the purpose of your message and then start thinking about other things. Like how you don't really need rooms for a gas station like you do in a home.

Each of us has a very different rationale to choose the objective. I had explained this in the beginning of the book as well. We are like chefs. We are free to apply our own creativity to the process of cooking a dish by following a recipe or a step by step guide to making of that dish. It is important we follow the recipe and stick to the ingredients as much as possible.

Coming back to the corporate scenario we discussed in the beginning of the chapter, let us study the objectives for the 5-minute presentation. If I were you, I would take the AEIOU Xtra E framework and draw the following six boxes on a paper. Now do this simple exercise. Take the eight objectives I listed above and ask yourself, which of these are SMART—specific, precise, achievable, realistic,, and time-bound.

Objective	SMART (Yes/No)
To give an update to the staff on the various data models you have analysed	No
To show 3 slides and speak for 5 minutes	Yes
To impress the staff with your analytical skills and articulation of the problem	No
To leave them with 2-3 main points they can remember that impact the business	Yes

Objective	SMART (Yes/No)
To make them feel good and make their 5 minutes worthwhile	No
To have a good time and enjoy the presentation	No
To engage and interact with the staff, answer their questions satisfactorily	No
To have simple slides—more visuals than text	No

Table 1: Identify if the objective is SMART or not

As you can see, things are a little clearer now. We can measure two out of eight points with a benchmark called SMART. And they become our starting points to craft our message. Each of you can do your own versions as well. Now, here is an important point. I am not saying that points 1, 3, 5, 6, 7 and 8 should not be included as your objectives because they are not SMART. But since it is difficult to benchmark them or measure them, our message might get confusing as well. So I will probably give more focus on the points 2 and 4 as compared to the others. It's like changing 'Abki Baar, Modi Sarkar' to 'Abki baar, change laao yaar'. The words 'Modi Sarkaar' are specific, precise, achievable, realistic, and time-bound. The words 'change laao yaar' do not pass the same test. However, they may be important too and you should keep them in the back of your mind while crafting your message which we will attempt in the next few chapters.

So now, fill the box called 'Objective' with your 2 SMART objectives so that it looks like below:

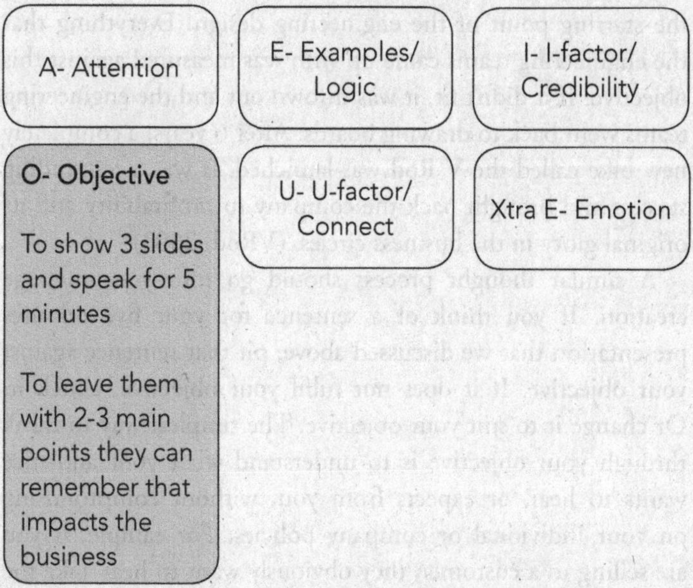

Figure 1: Fill the O of the AEIOU Xtra E framework

Congratulations! You now have a starting point to craft your message. Before we go any further, let's discuss why we need to have a SMART objective. It's a fair question. I will give you an example from the world of business. Any company which makes a product has an objective for that product. Harley Davidson was a monopoly in America till the early 80s before the Japanese and German bike manufacturers launched sleek and fast machines that ate into their market share. The traditional Harley was bulky and huge. The company was on the brink of collapse by the late 90s. They roped in the grandson of one of the founders who brought in a completely new philosophy for making a bike. He laid the objective of the project as 'the bike has to be fast like a low-rider model, look sleek, stylish and yet feel and sound like a Harley'. It had never been done before and became the starting point of the engineering design. Everything that the engineering teams came up with was measured against this objective. If it didn't fit, it was thrown out and the engineering teams went back to drawing boards. After 6 years, a completely new bike called the V Rod was launched. It was a resounding success and brought back the company to profitability and its original glory in the business circles. (VRod, 2003)

A similar thought process should go into your message creation. If you think of a sentence for your five minutes presentation that we discussed above, pit that sentence against your objective. If it does not fulfil your objective, chuck it. Or change it to suit your objective. The simplest way to think through your objective is to understand what your audience wants to hear, or expects from you, without compromising on your individual or company policies. For eample, if you are selling to a customer, they obviously want to hear 'take the product free' from you. But you cannot do that as it is against the company policy. But if you think hard, the customer wants to hear 'what is the benefit of your product to me/us'. And if you can now craft your message around that objective, you might reach a good outcome. Here is a table to define Ajay's objectives from an audience point of view.

What does your audience want to hear?	SMART (Yes/ No)	Is it possible for you to do it?
I want to get 2-3 key points that I can use in my business operations.	Yes	Yes
I don't want to see slides that have charts and numbers which I don't understand.	No	NA

What does your audience want to hear?	SMART (Yes/No)	Is it possible for you to do it?
I expect this person to know how to analyse data and articulate the problem in a way that I can understand.	No	NA
I want him to answer my questions satisfactorily. If he is not able to do so in that meeting due to lack of time or information, then at least he should be able to understand the question and help in getting the answer later.	No	NA
I want to see an energetic, passionate young person who likes his job by the way they present.	No	NA
I am giving him 5 minutes of my time. I hope it's worth it.	No	NA

Table 2: What the audience wants to hear

So you can see that the objective you have charted for yourself in Table 1 is similar to what the audience expects from you. This means that it is a good objective and you can now move to the next step of crafting the message. All we are doing is applying some basic tools to ensure that we are in the right direction.

Exercises

Let's do some more exercises to make our understanding of the concept better.

1. Imagine you are a budding entrepreneur who makes designer hoodies for college students customized for their colleges. You have a meeting with the dean of the college and have to present him your products. What is the objective of your meeting? Apply both tables and the AEIOU Xtra E box methods.

2. You are the project manager for a critical product of an IT company. Your team has slipped the delivery schedule by 2 weeks and your customer is very upset. You have a meeting with their CEO and his team to explain why the delay happened and what are the next steps. What is the objective of your meeting? Apply both tables and the AEIOU Xtra E box methods.

Chapter 6

Building Credibility—The I-Factor

We have discussed the crucial role the audience plays in passing judgement on how a leader articulates. It is very important that a speaker satisfactorily answers all these questions in the information that he presents to the audience

1. What do you want from me
2. **Who are you**
3. Why should I agree with you/Prove your point (Convince me)
4. What's in it for me
5. How do I act on the things you are asking me to do

In this chapter we will discuss how to successfully address the question '**Who are you**'.

Imagine you are walking on the street. A young man approaches you and offers you a biscuit and says 'eat it'. You don't know him from Adam. Will you eat it? Chances are that you will not even take that biscuit and possibly ignore the person completely. Why is that? I think it's because we don't trust this person. After all, what idea do we have about his intentions? We are bound to be suspicious of the unknown. Also the rising crime rate and the tales which accompany it make the situation even dodgier. So the lack of trust premised upon not knowing anything about the person is the main reason for not eating the biscuit. On a scale of 1 to 10, perhaps your trust in the stranger is at 1.

Now alter the situation a bit. Imagine that this young man shows you his ID card and says that he is from a recognized biscuit manufacturing company—say Britannia. You know it's a famous company. He shows you an official poster of the company with a letter from the CEO stating that they are doing test marketing for a biscuit. He also shows you approvals of the local food authorities department. He gives you his card which says 'Manager Marketing, Britannia'. On a scale of 1 to 10, it's possible that your trust will now be 9 or 10. Chances are that you *might* accept the biscuit. The chances are definitely better, but there is no guarantee that you will accept this biscuit. We will discuss this in the next chapter where the audience's question 'why should I agree with you' will be answered.

The same principle applies in persuading or influencing someone to get what you want. Your message has a better chance at succeeding if the audience knows you and trusts you. This is the Credibility or the I-factor of the AEIOU Xtra X framework. This aspect of demonstrating credibility to your audience is important, although a little tricky. There is a fine line between establishing trust and using power play to your advantage. And many times, we don't see that line and cross over to the other side. Here's an example. Assume you work for a manager who does not hesitate to use his power when he speaks with you or writes to you. It's a beautiful Friday evening and you are looking forward to the weekend. It's 5 pm and you are meeting your girlfriend for a movie and a dinner date at 7 pm. An email arrives to wreak havoc with your plans. It's from Bossman. You freeze. You have no choice but to open it as the office hours are till 6 pm. And you know that he will anyway wander by your office and ask 'hey did you check my email?' just to ensure that you respond NOW.

Here is what is in the mail

From: Bossman
To: YouTheSlave
Subject: Call with top customer at 6 pm. Urgent.
We have an urgent call with Mr The Customer at 6 pm. Please come to my office. We can conference with him from my phone.

You respond at 5.01 pm

From: YouTheSlave
To: Bossman
Boss, I have some personal urgent work at 7 pm. Can't we postpone to Monday?

You are expecting a reply any moment. And realize that Bossman has walked up to your cubicle. He doesn't look too happy and says, 'YouTheSlave, this is a very important call. As your manager of the project, I need you to stay'.

You are crestfallen. The words 'as the manager of the project' did the damage. You see the power play of Bossman and are left with no choice. You text your girlfriend that you can't make it and silently curse the Bossman. It won't be too surprising if you contemplate leaving the job. This is quite common in the corporate world and even beyond it. As parents, we often indulge in power play with our children as well, especially when we make statements like 'I am your father and I am telling you this for your own good.' Delhi is notorious for characters who field a version of the 'Do you know who my daddy is' whenever they have a run-in with the law.

Credibility is a double-edged sword. If you demonstrate less of it, the audience doesn't trust you. If you do it more, it might sound boastful to your audiences and they might switch off. Whatever be the case, remember this—**Thou shalt demonstrate your Credibility to your audience if the situation demands you to**. Why, you ask? As I mentioned earlier, the audience doesn't know you. Or has possibly forgotten you.

So what is credibility and how does one measure it? Credibility is defined as introducing yourself to your audience so that they start trusting you. Credibility is like a linear scale on which your audiences can rate the trust they have in you. It is a perceived quality, one that people assign to you based on the interplay of a number of elements. (Budzowski, N.D.). Let's take a closer look at the various dimensions of credibility that an audience looks out for.

Dimensions of credibility

1. **Expertise** or **competence**: Research on how viewers of news on television make or change opinions show that opinion changes significantly if the person speaking on TV is venerated as an expert. (Cialdini, 2001). There is a better chance of people accepting the views of an expert or take them seriously. For example, your chances of accepting a theory in class are a lot higher if you know that the professor has written many books on that topic and is a well-known expert. On the contrary, if the same theory is taught by a young student doing his PhD under the expert, you might question it or dismiss it. You might even go and complain to the dean of the university saying that you are spending a fortune to study under the best professors and don't want non-experts like the research assistants or the PhD students substituting for the teachers. Your educational qualification and designation are important ways to establish your credibility for your

audience. Other factors adding to the I-factor could be awards you have received or books you have published.

2. **Integrity**: There is a well-known story of Gandhi and the child who was addicted to jaggery. The child's father took him to Gandhi to talk him out of his habit of eating jaggery. The father thought that Gandhi's sheer stature would do the trick and the awestruck child would do as he was told. Gandhi however asked them to come back after two weeks. The father was puzzled but did not dare to argue. He returned with the boy after two weeks and met Gandhi. This time, Gandhi said to the child, 'Son, don't eat jaggery. It's not good for you.' The father couldn't help saying, 'Bapu, you could have said the same sentence two weeks ago. Why didn't you?' Gandhi replied, 'Two weeks ago, I also used to eat jaggery. How can I preach to your son to stop eating it when I myself did the same? So I took two weeks to cease my own habit and then talk to your son.' This simple story really shows how honesty in a leader is the simplest trait that audiences respect. A leader with high integrity will move his or her audience more easily than one whose integrity is either unknown or questionable. Nobody believes a liar. Just as with the boy who cried wolf, your audiences will never listen to you if you deceive them once. In today's age, people are 'googling' their leaders all the time. Idea, the mobile network operator, is airing an ad which demonstrates how people can no longer be taken for a ride as they have smartphones and access to internet. In one of the ads, a leader is giving a speech during elections. A small boy uses the cell phone to Google his past record and exposes his less than stellar reputation. 'No ooloo banaoing' is the punch line of these ads which roughly translates to 'don't fool your audience'. The message is quite clear. If

you want your audience to trust you, they should have no doubt on your integrity. There are examples where top leaders have had to step down because of falsified resumes. The most famous one is the ouster of Yahoo CEO Scott Thomson because his resume was fudged. (Brooks, 2012)

3. **Character**: A speaker who is considered morally upright has a greater chance of persuading an audience. A perfect example could be the case of Tiger Woods. His personal life was considered picture perfect. He was successfully endorsing many brands. But the day the media brought his sexual escapades to light and his wife publicly left him for good, his stars fell. He lost his brand endorsements and his career graph dipped to a new low.
4. **Track record**: Nothing speaks louder than the past performances of an individual. You look at any job interview or selection procedure for any award. The prior track record of the individual speaks volumes and qualifies them to the next stage. Would Steve Jobs inspire so many if he hadn't launched successful products like the Mac and its versions? Let me quiz you—name the first person to scale Mount Everest. Chances are very high that you will nail the answer—Edmund Hillary. Now if I ask you, who the second or the third persons were, you probably won't know. It's quite natural. We love winners and winning. And when we are an audience, we like to see winners as well. We trust them more. So the more successful you are in your work or in a certain category, the more trust your audience will bestow on you. The name E. Sreedharan is legendary in India. He is also called the Metro Man of India. He is credited for successfully executing the Konkan Railway project and then also the Metro Rail project in Delhi. He had to coordinate various departments and agencies in that job which was not easy. Now, if he has to

make a speech on project management, the audience will be inclined to trust his words more because of how he has delivered in the past.

5. **Appearance/style or confidence:** Imagine what impact Gandhi's words would have had if he wore spectacular Saville Row suits like Jinnah, spoke about nationalism, and asked people to boycott English products. Gandhi was educated in the UK, worked in South Africa, but knew that his audience in India didn't even have food to eat and clothes to wear. One of the reasons the Indian audience trusted him was because of how he dressed and chose to live. It is said, if you want to look successful, dress accordingly. How you appear says a lot about you to your audience. Just try going to a top management meeting in a country like Germany or the middle-east without a tie and a jacket. Or try entering a club in Bangalore in flip-flops. Appearance matters and it helps build credibility. The audience trusts you more when you appear confident. The way you walk, the way you stand, the way you dress, the way you shake hands, combined with your track record and the style of your communication creates an aura which is called your Executive Presence. (Hewlett, 2014)
6. **Demographics:** This is somewhat contextual but worth mentioning here. The audience might be interested in knowing your lineage, age, gender, caste, background, and various other demographic aspects. For this you will have to use your own discretion and tackle the audience accordingly.

Besides the above, there are various other minor aspects that can influence the level of trust the audience has in you. They depend on the kind of culture that you belong to. For example, in Asian cultures like China and India, there is a lot of emphasis on power. So your designation would carry weight there. Some cultures value educational qualification more and some measure credibility by the wealth of the speaker. Countries like Japan give importance to age and experience as an important measure of credibility. On my recent visit to the US, I met many young. bright people. One of these introduced himself as, 'Hi, I am Raj. I started two companies and both failed. I am now starting a third venture.' I asked him why he would explicitly say that his ventures failed. Didn't that dilute his credibility and track record? 'Not at all,' Ajay responded. 'In fact, it shows that I am a risk taker and have a track record of starting new ventures. Many VCs in the US value this quality.' When he said this, I asked him, 'Would you introduce yourself in a similar fashion to an audience in India?' And he said, 'No. I will probably not mention the failure part. Audiences in India don't consider ability to fail as a good trait in an entrepreneur.' So as I mentioned, cultures play an important role in how you establish credibility with your audiences.

BARACK OBAMA: THE AUDACITY OF HOPE

Barack Obama was a senator from Illinois, USA and mostly unknown in the world till 2007 when he declared his candidature to run for President of USA. I remember watching CNN where they randomly asked people in the US, 'Do you know Obama?' and many of them answered in negative. Just imagine the odds present in front of this man when he dreamed of becoming the president of USA. He wasn't born in USA. He is not white and not many people knew him in his own state of Illinois, forget an entire country. However, he gradually built his credibility using his messages that he gave in various forums and presence in the media. I am outlining some sentences from his speeches from 2004 and 2007. (Obama, 2009). Note how well he answers the simple questions of the audience and how his responses adhere to the various dimensions of credibility I have mentioned above. If I was a US citizen these could be some of my doubts on his candidature.

1. Are you an American or a Kenyan?
2. Are you a Christian?
3. What is your qualification?
4. What makes you think that you can be president?

> As most of you know, I am not a native of this great state. I moved to Illinois over two decades ago. I was a young man then, just a year out of college; I knew no one in Chicago, was without money or family connections.
>
> It was in these neighborhoods that I received the best education I ever had, and where I learned the true meaning of my Christian faith.
>
> After three years of this work, I went to law school, because I wanted to understand how the law should work for those in need. I became a civil rights lawyer, and taught constitutional law, and after a time, I came to understand that our cherished rights of liberty and equality depend on the active participation of an awakened electorate. It was with these ideas in mind that I arrived in this capital city as a state Senator.
>
> And I accepted the job, sight unseen, motivated then by a single, simple, powerful idea—that I might play a small part in building a better America.

This speech that he gave on 10 February, 2007 is a follow-up to his earlier speeches. Each of them built his credibility step by step. He tells the American audience that, 'I am an

American and like you, I want a better country.' In 2004 at the Democratic National Convention, asking the American people to vote for John Kerry, he cemented his credibility with the American audience. Here are some excerpts.

> Tonight is a particular honour for me because, let's face it, my presence on this stage is pretty unlikely. My father was a foreign student, born and raised in a small village in Kenya. He grew up herding goats, went to school in a tin-roof shack. His father, my grandfather, was a cook, a domestic servant.
>
> But my grandfather had larger dreams for his son. Through hard work and perseverance my father got a scholarship to study in a magical place: America, which stood as a beacon of freedom and opportunity to so many who had come before. While studying here, my father met my mother. She was born in a town on the other side of the world, in Kansas. Her father worked on oil rigs and farms through most of the Depression. The day after Pearl Harbor he signed up for duty, joined Patton's army and marched across Europe. Back home, my grandmother raised their baby and went to work on a bomber assembly line. After the war, they studied on the GI Bill, bought a house through FHA, and moved west in search of opportunity.
>
> And they, too, had big dreams for their daughter, a common dream, born of two continents. My parents shared not only an improbable love; they shared an abiding faith in the possibilities of this nation. They would give me an African name, Barack, or 'blessed', believing that in a tolerant America your name is no barrier to success. They imagined me going to the best schools in the land, even

> though they weren't rich, because in a generous America you don't have to be rich to achieve your potential. They are both passed away now. Yet, I know that, on this night, they look down on me with pride.

The words demonstrate all the dimensions of credibility that I pointed out earlier. He spoke of his lineage, his family history, his roots, his expertise, integrity, character, and track record. Remember one thing—never expect the audience to know everything about you. Your job is to demonstrate your credibility, to ensure that the audience trusts you and does what you want them to do. So don't shy away from talking about yourself without sounding too boastful.

If you look at the photographs of Barack Obama in a book called *The Rise of Barack Obama* complied by a photographer Pete Souza, you will find his dressing style simple, but impeccable. He looks confident, tall, and fit. No wonder he was and still is a very popular leader. Appearance and looks do matter. But more than that it's the positive image you project that works in your favour. (Souza, 2010)

Here are some more examples of sentences from TED talks I collected which demonstrate the I-factor or credibility. (TED, 2014)

S no.	Actual sentence spoken	Dimension of credibility demonstrated
1.	I have worked with more than 500 companies in the last 10 years.	Expertise/ competence

S no.	Actual sentence spoken	Dimension of credibility demonstrated
2.	Now, being Iranian-American presents its own set of problems, as you know.	Demographics
3.	We started with 25000 passengers a day few years ago, now it's 2200000 passengers a day.	Track record
4.	I am in charge of making this country's food secure.	Expertise through power/ designation
5.	This slide sums up thousands of pages of technical documents that we have been working on over past 2 years.	Expertise through knowledge
6.	This is a picture of me and my three children.	Appearance
7.	I did my PhD from MIT where I focused on…	Expertise through qualification
8.	I must confess that I did not play a big role here. It was my team.	Integrity
9.	I was asked to do something that I did not believe in. So I quit.	Character

Table 1: Examples of sentences that demonstrate credibility

Let's now take the example of our young MBA graduate Ajay who had been asked to give a 5 minute update in the staff meeting to the CEO and his direct reports that we discussed in the previous chapter. In that chapter, we used the AEIOU Xtra E framework and completed the Objective. Now let's fill the I-Factor or the Credibility box.

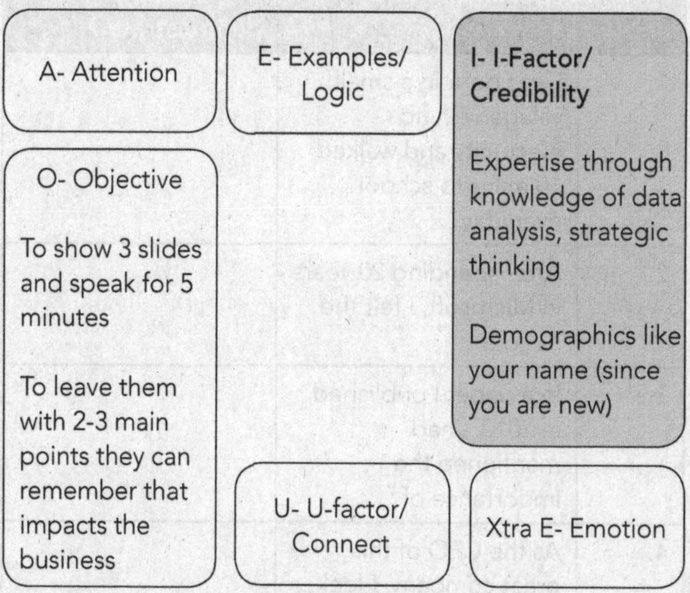

Figure 1: Fill the I of the AEIOU Xtra E framework

Exercise

1. What are the dimensions of credibility that you can identify in the statements below?

S no.	Actual Sentence spoken/written	Dimension of credibility demonstrated
1.	I was born in a small village with no electricity and walked 10 miles to school everyday.	
2.	After spending 20 years in Microsoft, I felt the need of…	
3.	In a paper I published in 2010, I had mentioned the importance of…	
4.	As the CEO of this great company, I feel…	
5.	Every year, we have demonstrated a record growth of 8 percent.	
6.	Though I may not have much hair left on my head and don't look like Brad Pitt…	

S no.	Actual Sentence spoken/written	Dimension of credibility demonstrated
7.	Once I graduated from IIM Bangalore, a top B School in India, I came to London.	
8.	I am William Wallace.	

CHAPTER 7

Explaining the Logic to Your Audience

AS WE DISCUSSED IN CHAPTER 4, the audience decides the success of a message. In this chapter we learn how to explain the logic to our audience—which forms the E of our framework. The audience assesses the merits and the demerits of a message on the basis of the following parameters.

1. What do you want from me
2. Who are you
3. Why should I agree with you/Prove your point (Convince me)
4. What's in it for me
5. How do I act on the things you are asking me to do

In this chapter we will discuss how to address the question '**Why should I agree with you**'.

In the example of a man approaching you with a biscuit and asking you to eat it, we discussed how you would not take that biscuit and ignore the person because of your lack of trust. Once the trust is established, the audience will have many more doubts and questions in their minds before they make a final decision. Every person is unique and therefore the kind of question would differ from person to person. Some of these doubts and questions could possibly be

1. Why should I eat it?
2. What is it made of?
3. What is so special about this biscuit?

The key to successful persuasion are the critical tools of logic and explanation from the sender of the message to his audiences. The speaker (sender) has to understand the mind of the audience, read their attitude and ensure that the message is logical and the audience will be able to understand it. This logic and understanding fuels their trust in you and brings them closer to a decision. Again, there is still no guarantee that the person *will* eat the biscuit. But it definitely increases the rate of success.

Explanation of the topic is a key pillar of the rhetorical theory proposed by Aristotle more than 2300 years ago. (Kennedy, 1991). (Rapp, 2010).The basic premise of a sound explanation is to ensure that the audience understands the topic which helps them come closer to taking the action. Our brain has 2 halves that process information differently. They are also popularly known as the left and right brain. The left part is very analytical and the right part is intuitive. The left brain processes numbers, facts and hard data and the right part processes emotions, visuals, diagrams etc. (UCMAS, 2007). And we use both the halves to understand and perceive the world. As a speaker we need to satisfy both halves. In this chapter we will focus on the logical half of the audiences' brain. And later, we will look at the emotional part separately.

Providing logic to your audience

Logic stems from philosophy and might take a lifetime to understand. Logic underlies Mathematics, Science, and Technology as well. (Pittsburg, 2007). Sherlock Holmes is a much-loved character who uses logic in a unique way to solve mysteries. The creator of Sherlock Holmes, Sir Arthur Conan Doyle, presents a perplexing crime or a very strange predicament in every story. Our friend, Mr Holmes, has a unique way of identifying the real culprit in a way that escapes most people's notice—even the police's. Holmes presents the same facts in a very different pattern, combined with new reasoning and evidence to support his argument. Facts in themselves are useless sometimes. It's the way they are explained to the audiences that makes the difference in persuasion. (Tindale, 2004)

Richard Feynman used to say that if you can't explain something to others in the simplest possible way, you probably don't understand it yourself. His friend Leonard Susskind made a wonderful statement in his TED talk on Richard Feynman, he said the best way to honour Feynman was to cut as much 'baloney in your sandwiches as possible' or in simple words 'make things as simple for others to understand'. (Leonard Susskind: My friend Richard Feynman, 2011). Here are few ways that you can provide good explanations so that the audience understands them better.

1. Tell stories that convey the logic

In a wonderful article written by Leo Wildrich, founder of Buffer, he explains why stories are so impactful on audiences.

> For over 27,000 years, since the first cave paintings were discovered, telling stories has been one of our most fundamental communication methods. A story can put your whole brain to work. We all enjoy a good story, whether it's a novel, a movie, or simply something one of our friends is explaining to us. But why do we feel so much more engaged when we hear a narrative about events?

It's in fact quite simple. If we listen to a powerpoint presentation with boring bullet points, a certain part in the brain gets activated. Scientists call this Broca's Area and Wernicke's Area. Overall, it hits our language processing parts of the brain, where we decode words into meaning. And that's it, nothing else happens.

When we are being told a story, things change dramatically. Not only are the language processing parts in our brain activated, but any other area in our brain that we would use when experiencing the events of the story are too. (Wildrich, 2012)

One of the best examples of how stories can help a speaker make greater impact on his audience is the famous 'Stay hungry stay foolish' speech by Steve Jobs at the Stanford convocation in 2005. We all know him as an inventor, a maverick businessman, and the God of revolutionary technological innovation. He is famous for his rousing and motivating speeches. This 2005 speech has been quoted by scholars and academicians as well to demonstrate how stories can be a powerful tool to convey a message to your audience. In his thought-provoking speech, Jobs lay down three simple messages to the graduating class of Stanford through stories from his own life. Here are some excerpts from his speech. (Yarrow, 2011). You can also check out the entire video on TED or YouTube. (Steve Jobs Commencement speech at Stanford, 2005)

Today I want to tell you three stories from my life. That's it. No big deal. Just three stories.

The first story is about connecting the dots.

I dropped out of Reed College after the first 6 months, but then stayed around as a drop-in for another 18 months or so before I really quit. So why did I drop out?

He goes on to tell the story for 3-4 minutes and despite being very descriptive, it commands rapt attention.

> None of this had even a hope of any practical application in my life. But ten years later, when we were designing the first Macintosh computer, it all came back to me. And we designed it all into the Mac. It was the first computer with beautiful typography. If I had never dropped in on that single course in college, the Mac would have never had multiple typefaces or proportionally spaced fonts. And since Windows just copied the Mac, it's likely that no personal computer would have them. If I had never dropped out, I would have never dropped in on this calligraphy class, and personal computers might not have the wonderful typography that they do now. Of course it was impossible to connect the dots looking forward when I was in college. But it was very, very clear looking backwards ten years later.
>
> Again, you can't connect the dots looking forward; you can only connect them looking backwards. So you have to trust that the dots will somehow connect in your future. You have to trust in something—your gut, destiny, life, karma, whatever. This approach has never let me down, and it has made all the difference in my life.

The third story that he narrated made his words almost immortal. This is how it goes.

> When I was young, there was an amazing publication called *The Whole Earth Catalog*, which was one of the bibles of my generation. It was created by a fellow named Stewart Brand, who lived not far from here in Menlo

Park. He brought it to life with his poetic touch. This was in the late 1960's, before personal computers and desktop publishing, so it was all made with typewriters, scissors, and Polaroid cameras. It was sort of like Google in paperback form, 35 years before Google came along: it was idealistic, and overflowing with neat tools and great notions.

Stewart and his team put out several issues of The Whole Earth Catalog, and then when it had run its course, they put out a final issue. It was the mid-1970s, and I was your age. On the back cover of their final issue was a photograph of an early morning country road, the kind you might find yourself hitchhiking on if you were any bit adventurous. Beneath it were the words: 'Stay Hungry. Stay Foolish.' It was their farewell message as they signed off. Stay Hungry. Stay Foolish. And I have always wished that for myself. And now, as you graduate to begin anew, I wish that for you.

Stay Hungry. Stay Foolish.

Thank you all very much.

The simplest form of storytelling technique is a narrative or an anecdote which the speaker can relate with ample detail to transport his or her audiences. (Denning, 2004). Once the stage is set, the story has to highlight a problem or a plot clearly. The narrative should compel the audience to wonder 'what will happen next' or 'what would I do in such a situation'. When the time is right, the speaker then reveals the 'Aha! moment' and starts nudging the audience towards the solution and finally connects this to the objective of the talk. Read Steve Jobs' speech one more time and see how effortlessly he follows this 5-step approach.

i. Start with the objective
ii. Build the story with a timeline, details, setting, place, protagonist, characters, context—anything you feel is required for the story
iii. Take your audience to that world and let them see the 'problem' clearly
iv. Explain how the protagonist solved the problem
v. Connect the story with your objective and bring it to a closure

One can even use metaphors, similes, quotations, poems, or examples to drive home the point if you are not comfortable with storytelling or if the situation doesn't allow you to. Written forms of communication like emails and letters are such opportunities where metaphors, similies, quotes and examples are more suitable. In 2011, Nokia was not doing too well. They were almost swept away by the success of the iPhone and Android phones. Rumour was that the company was up for grabs. The markets had written them off. In these circumstances, the CEO of Nokia Stephen Elop wrote a letter to his entire team worldwide. He uses an example of a man on a burning platform in the middle of a sea to convey Nokia's situation metaphorically. His email conveyed that something drastic would happen soon. Here are some sentences of his email that fit the first 3 steps mentioned in the framework above. (Elop, 2011)

> There is a pertinent story about a man who was working on an oil platform in the North Sea. He woke up one night from a loud explosion, which suddenly set his entire oil platform on fire. In mere moments, he was surrounded by flames. Through the smoke and heat, he barely made

his way out of the chaos to the platform's edge. When he looked down over the edge, all he could see were the dark, cold, foreboding Atlantic waters.

As the fire approached him, the man had mere seconds to react. He could stand on the platform, and inevitably be consumed by the burning flames. Or, he could plunge 30 meters in to the freezing waters. The man was standing upon a 'burning platform', and he needed to make a choice.

He decided to jump. It was unexpected. In ordinary circumstances, the man would never consider plunging into icy waters. But these were not ordinary times—his platform was on fire. The man survived the fall and the waters. After he was rescued, he noted that a 'burning platform' caused a radical change in his behaviour.

We too, are standing on a 'burning platform,' and we must decide how we are going to change our behaviour.

Elop's message did not have points iv and v at all. That's possibly because he didn't already have a solution. It seems he wanted to sound the alarm. Well, Microsoft finally did buy out the handset division of Nokia and together, they are now on their way to deliver Windows and Android phones for the market. That was probably the jump into the icy sea that Elop was hinting at.

Another useful example of how one can make intelligent use of metaphors, similes and quotations in a message is Martin Luther King's famous speech 'I have a dream'. Throughout this historical speech, King uses a lot of rhetorical instruments of storytelling and wins his audience around the world. Here are some of my favorite sections from his speech. (King, 1963)

> I have a dream that one day, down in Alabama, with its vicious racists, with its governor having his lips dripping with the words of 'interposition' and 'nullification'—one day right there in Alabama little black boys and black girls will be able to join hands with little white boys and white girls as sisters and brothers.

Here are some examples of how King uses metaphors. (Dlugan, 2012)

> 'joyous daybreak to end the long night of their captivity' [paragraph 2]
>
> 'the Negro lives on a lonely island of poverty in the midst of a vast ocean of material prosperity' [3]
>
> 'rise from the dark and desolate valley of segregation to the sunlit path of racial justice' [6]
>
> 'This sweltering summer of the Negro's legitimate discontent will not pass until there is an invigorating autumn of freedom and equality.' [7]
>
> 'sweltering with the heat of oppression, will be transformed into an oasis of freedom and justice.' [19]

Interspersing your speech with mythological stories, and even everyday stories, is an interesting technique. A good example could be Mani Shankar Aiyar's story on the food security bill that was published in the *Hindu*. This is how the first paragraph of that story begins, drawing from Greek mythology. (Aiyar, 2012)

> In ancient Greece, the punishment given to Tantalus was to tie a cup around his neck and fill it with water. Every time he bent to take a sip, the cup would drop further

> and he would never get a drop into his parched mouth. From this comes the word 'tantalizing'. Something like that is happening with food security. However much food we procure and at whatever expense, not till what has been procured, stored and transported reaches the final consumer would the consumer have anything other than the cup of Tantalus tied around his neck.

The title of the article was 'Food security and the cup of Tantalus'. Aiyar's core objective was to convey this message, 'the key issue is not availability or resources, but last mile delivery: how to get food grains to the people.' In just a paragraph, Aiyar managed to highlight the problem clearly by showing the audience the vision of Tantalus and the pain of his predicament. In the rest of the article, he went on to suggest various ways to combat the problem—the food security bill that his party was pushing in the parliament. So he endeavoured to shape public opinion by cleverly using a story rather than complicated facts and figures.

Here's another example of a piece that Paul Krugman, a professor of Economics at Princeton University, and popular financial columnist, wrote on the world's economic situation in 2011. This was the year when many countries declared 'austerity' measures after many companies went bankrupt, the global markets crashed, and the US and Europe economies announced that they were officially in depression. Austerity drive was a measure to reduce expenditure and promote frugality, to stay afloat during the sweeping economic crisis. So here is what Krugman wrote in the article 'The Bleeding Cure'. (Krugman, 2011)

> Doctors used to believe that by draining a patient's blood they could purge the evil 'humours' that were thought to

> cause disease. In reality, of course, all their bloodletting did was make the patient weaker, and more likely to succumb. Fortunately, physicians no longer believe that bleeding the sick will make them healthy. Unfortunately, many of the makers of economic policy still do. And economic bloodletting isn't just inflicting vast pain; it's starting to undermine our long-run growth prospects.
>
> Some background: For the past year and a half, policy discourse in both Europe and the United States has been dominated by calls for fiscal austerity. By slashing spending and reducing deficits, we were told, nations could restore confidence and drive economic revival.

He goes on to elaborate how this is hurting everyone and in the end nudges the policy makers in another direction, suggesting another solution.

> What we really need, however, is to convince a substantial number of people with political power or influence that they've spent the last year and a half going in exactly the wrong direction, and that they need to make a U-turn.

I chanced upon a website which gave examples of how the world's poorest President Jose 'Pepe' Mujica, who is known for his frank and fiery oration and simple lifestyle. This website gave his views on various topics ranging from economic policies to gay marriage. (Mascarenhas, 2014). Each of these quotes are great examples how he uses metaphors, stories, and anecdotes to convey his point to the audiences. When he was asked of his view on abortion and same-sex marriages he said

> We applied a very simple principle: Recognize the facts. Abortion is old as the world. Gay marriage, please — it's older than the world. We had Julius Caesar, Alexander the

Great. To say it's modern, come on, it's older than we are. It's an objective reality that it exists. For us, not legalizing it would be to torture people needlessly.

Let's now take the example of Ajay, our young MBA graduate who has been asked to give a 5 minute update in the next staff meeting to the CEO and his direct reports that we discussed in earlier chapter. In the last chapter, we used the AEIOU Xtra E framework and completed the I-factor/Credibility box. Now let's fill the examples box.

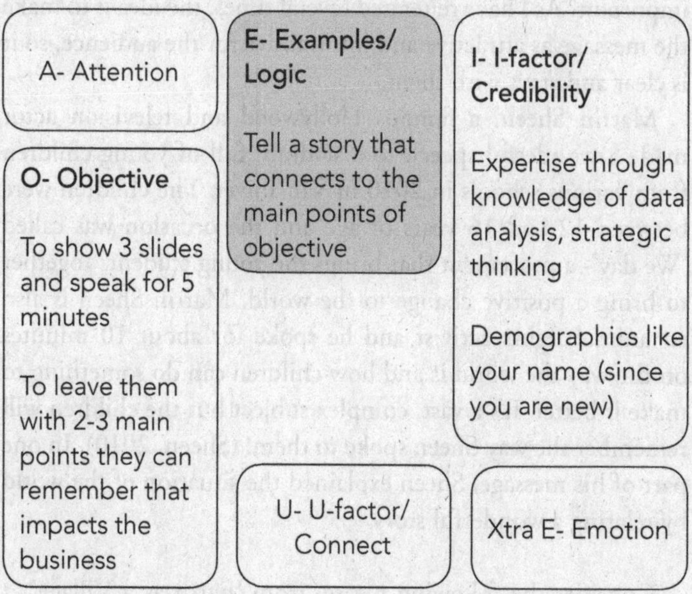

Figure 1: Fill the example box of the AEIOU Xtra E framework

2. *Make data interesting and fun*

A critical element of logic is verifiable facts and data which supports your argument. The world runs on numbers to understand logic and there is no way one can avoid them. The hottest job in the corporate world at an entry level is 'business analyst' and it involves interpreting data and making some sense out of it to make an informed business decision. Our friend, Ajay, the MBA, who is about to make the presentation to the CEO staff will definitely need to work on this aspect.

So how does one make data interesting and fun for an audience? Well, it takes a little creativity and a whole lot of practice to do this. But once you crack it, all your talks and sessions—be it in corporate sector or even in regular socializing—will undergo a major transformation. And why is it important? As I have reiterated several times, the idea is to make the message as attractive and informative for the audience, so it is clear and stays with them.

Martin Sheen, a famous Hollywood and television actor made a wonderful speech to a stadium full of young children from various schools in 2010 in Vancouver. The children were between 12 and 16 years of age and the occasion was called 'We day'- a movement that brings the young students together to bring a positive change to the world. Martin Sheen is also an animal rights activist and he spoke for about 10 minutes on the way the world is and how children can do something to make it better. It's a vast, complex subject but the children will remember the way Sheen spoke to them. (Sheen, 2010). In one part of his message, Sheen explained the situation of the world by relating a wonderful story.

> Consider the following please, from 'Earth as a Village' by Phillips M. Harter, Stanford school of medicine. If we could shrink the earth's population of over six and a half billion people down to a single village consisting of one hundred people, with all the existing races the same, it would look something like this; there would be 57 Asians, 8 Europeans 21 Africans and 14 people from the

western hemisphere. There would be 52 women and 48 men. There would be 70 non-white and 30 white. There would be 70 non-Christians and 30 Christians, there would be no doctor, no nurse, no dentist, no hospital or clinic and no school, there would be no safe drinking water, there would be no common language, there would be no electricity and no paved roads, there would be 70 people unable to read or write, there would be 50 people suffering from malnutrition, there would be one person near death and one person near birth. The entire food supply for the village would depend entirely on outside sources. Six people on that village would possess 59 percent of the entire world's wealth and all 6 would be US citizens. There would be one collage graduate, one TV, one computer and the average person on that village would be a 13-year-old Chinese girl.

This passage that Sheen recounted to the children, from Harter's book *Earth as a Village,* simply but memorably explained the demographics of the world and the major problems we face today. I wouldn't be surprised if many students quoted those stats to others, and actually grow up to be more conscientious adults. If Sheen had not presented the facts so beautifully, he wouldn't have had such an impact on his audience.

Hans Rosling, a health expert and speaker on TED explains data beautifully through creative visuals and props. His profile on TED's website says that 'Data sings in his hands'. (TED.com, 2005). And you can see it for yourself in any one of his talks. In a talk he made in 2010, he showcased years of boring listless data from various agencies like United Nations, World Health Organization, Red Cross, etc and mesmerized his audience. They saw visuals that were lively and interesting rather than the usual graphs and charts that many of us see every day and took away useful information. (Rosling, 2010)

Here are some ways to present data. I am making a table where the same data is presented in two different ways. You decide which is more interesting to you. (APMYY, 2014)

India's road network is 4.7 million kilometers	India's road network is long enough to loop around the Earth over 117 times
India saw 138258 deaths in road accidents in 2012	One person died on the road in India every 3 minutes in 2012
Cherapunji gets 463.66 inches of rain every year	Cherapunji gets 40 feet of rain every year—that is about 6 Amitabh Bacchans put on top of each other
By 2020, the median age in India will be 29	India will become the youngest country by 2020
India consumed 1.2 billion liters of Whiskey in 2012	India consumed 1.2 billion liters of Whiskey in 2012—that is approximately the water that goes in 48 Olympic size swimming pools that is 50 meter long, 20 meter wide and 2 meter deep (PoolCalculator, 2014)
81 million hectares of land is facing desertification due to lack of rains in India	About 25 percent land of India is turning into a desert—that is the equivalent of 3 United Kingdoms

New Delhi air has PM or particulate matter of 2.5 micrometers or less which is harmful to lungs	Air in New Delhi is the most polluted and dangerous in the world
India has 275 billion tons of coal reserves	India has 275 billion tons of coal reserves. That's the equivalent of 1.37 billion blue whales put together

Table 1: Data presented in 2 different ways. Which is more interesting?

The second column would be preferred by most. This is because it's very simple to understand and the mind is able to visualize and contrast the information to something which it can relate to. For example, 275 billion tons of coal takes our mind to a coal mine, but when we contrast this to masses of blue whales, the impact is much higher. The audience finds it easier to remember such a visual—the recall is much higher. I remember when I was in Intel, one of our senior vice presidents included a funny slide whenever he presented the quarterly update. In one of those updates, there were three numbers on the slide—46 million, 20 million, 23. He asked what these numbers meant to us. We got the first one right—it was the number of transistors in the chip we were working on. The second was tough to crack. He said that that number was the equivalent of hair on his head now and joked that when he was younger, it was over 100 million. He pointed to his partially bald head and we all had a laugh. The third number was the number of years he spent at Intel. I can never forget the impact that slide had on me. It made me like him more than all the other leaders that had come before him.

Remember—compare and contrast your data with simple objects from everyday life that audience can relate to and which make your data more interesting to them.

So by now, our framework looks like this.

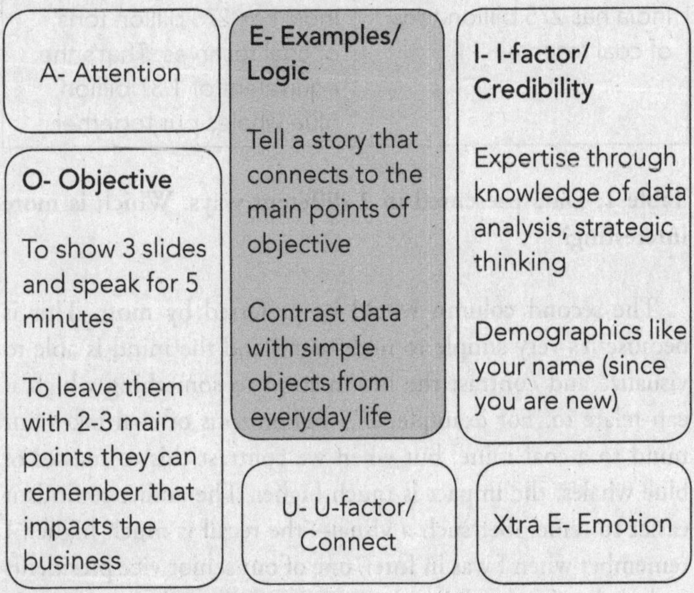

Figure 2 - Updated framework for explanation

Exercise

1. You are working for an NGO that helps in providing mid-day meals to children in schools. You are supposed to meet some high networth individuals and talk to them about the program and ask them to contribute Rs 1000 per month for 3 years—Rs 36000 overall.

   a. What is an appropriate story you will choose for your talk that fits our Example element in the AEIOU Xtra E framework
   b. Instead of a story, can you choose an example or anecdote instead
   c. Assume that your audience profile has members from the finance industry. They are bankers and people who understand numbers, statistics and complicated maths. They don't like stories or examples which have no numbers. But in the same room, you also have their spouses. How will you make your data in such a way that is interesting for both categories of the audience—the bankers and their spouses

CHAPTER 8

Connecting with Your Audience

AS WE DISCUSSED IN CHAPTER 4, the audience decides the success of your message. In this chapter we learn how to connect with the audience—this is the U (you) factor of the framework. A critical aspect of this law is the need for the audience to ask the following questions to you as a speaker of the message.

1. What do you want from me
2. Who are you
3. Why should I agree with you/Prove your point (Convince me)
4. **What's in it for me**
5. How do I act on the things you are asking me to do

In this chapter we will discuss how to address the question '**What's in it for me**'. Another way we can phrase this question is '**What does the audience want to hear?**'

There is a quote that says, 'Success' cannot be spelt without 'U'. Communicating effectively with the audience is based on similar logic. Unless the audience sees the benefit to them, they will resist listening to you. Let's face it, we are all selfish beings; we are almost reflexively drawn towards things that carry potential for our betterment. We choose what we want to hear. So, if the speaker is able to persuade us that listening to him is good for us, chances are high that we would pay close attention. The U box of the framework is the one that deals with this aspect. I call it the U-factor. It helps establish a connection between the speaker and the audience.

Let us look at a couple of simulations to understand the point I made above—'we choose what we want to hear'. If you visit a busy street or a train station, you will observe people walking past oblivious of each other, totally engrossed in their own worlds. I happened to find something similar at a busy junction near my house. I called to a few people, 'Excuse me, I need some help.' Some people ignored me or pretended to not hare heard. Then I dropped a handful of coins on the road and noted that a lot of people's attention was caught. They looked. Some even patted their pockets, to make sure it that it wasn't their money that had fallen out. Hard earned money is important to us. So the sound of money tinkering on the ground will make us stop and turn our focus to where the sound had come from. Hence we listen carefully. The same logic applies when you are in a company presentation. If the speaker is saying something that has no bearing to the audience or their work, they will probably flip Facebook pages on their smartphones. But the moment the boss or a customer starts to say something in that meeting, your ears, brain and every sensory nerve in the body will be rapt in attention because he has a very crucial role to play in your career which impacts you directly.

In simple words, your audiences will agree more with you if they see a direct benefit from you and your topic. Let me rephrase that sentence a little bit to put the spotlight on you as the conveyer of that message. Your audience will agree more with you if you can tune the topic to suit their benefits. Conger terms this relationship as shared benefits between both parties in an article he wrote called 'The Art of Persuasion' (Conger, 1998) where he says that this frame of reference is crucial for the audience to accept the message. We all do this every day without even knowing it. If you have kids you will understand what I mean. If you want to take the family to your favorite Indian place for dinner, chances are that your little kids would push you for a pizza instead. You want Indian and they want Pizza. So how do you solve this problem? Well, you connect with them first, and then try and get them to accept what you want. Here's how. You would say something like, 'So you want to have pizza? All right then. Let's go to this pizza place and pick your favorite pizza which you can eat in the car as we drive to Papa's favorite Indian place. How about that?' Chances are very high that your plan might succeed and you might get to eat your favorite Indian food, because you connected with what your children wanted and once they got that, they were cool to go any where you took them.

In many ways, if you manage to connect with the audience, more than half the battle is won. It's almost as if you need to please your audience in some way to get your point across. Another term used is negotiate, but I will steer away from this term in this book altogether as it is a very complex topic and might digress the focus. Let's keep the discussion very simple and understand the U-factor in AEIOU as a way to think about the benefit for your audience before you put your thought across. Some purists may call it bribery and sneer at the thought of pleasing one's audience. I don't agree with this view at all. Don't we all please our customers first, lure them through smooth talk, offer a benefit, and then sell them something that we want to? Don't we all promise to buy a chocolate for our child to make him accompany us to the department store? Don't we all say yes to our boss even if we don't agree with his views, win his confidence, and then try to convince him to see it our way? If the answer to most of the above is yes, then how hard can it be to apply the same logic to win over an audience whether it is in a boardroom, a kitchen, or any place under the sun?

The easiest way to achieve the U in the AEIOU framework is to say things that the audience wants to hear. Or at least try and balance what they want to hear with what you want to say comfortably. You need not say anything which offends your sensibilities or moralities as a person. It is a tightrope walk to maintain a perfect equilibrium between what your audience wants and what you want.

So how can you connect with your audience? Here are some simple ways that I will highlight using a recent speech that Prime Minister Narendra Modi gave at the launch of PSLV satellite on 30 June, 2014 to the ISRO scientists at Sriharikota. (Modi, 2014)

1. Acknowledge and appreciate the audience

The audience is giving their time to you. The simplest way to connect with them is by acknowledging their time and presence with a warm smile and a polite thank you. It is not only a demonstration of the courteousness and good etiquette, but also a gesture that draws your audience closer to you. Another good practice is to applaud their work and contributions. The first sentence that Modi spoke at that occasion did exactly that. Here is how he began his speech

> **My congratulations to our brilliant space scientists, and the Department of Space**; for yet another successful launch of the Polar Satellite Launch Vehicle! We have perfectly placed 5 satellites into their orbits 660 km above the Earth. This fills every Indian's heart with pride. And

> I can see it reflected in the joy and satisfaction on **your faces.**

The text in bold demonstrates how a speaker can use simple words to connect with his audience—in this case the scientists of ISRO and the rest of India. The audience demands attention and recognition. We all do. Modi used 'you' and 'your' to pepper his speech to show his appreciation for the scientists. And this made his talk a lot more endearing as well. I will talk about the role of emotions later in the book.

2. *Take names of the members in the audience*

Dale Carnegie in the classic *How to Win Friends and Influence People*, writes something that I can never forget. (Carnegie, 1936). He dedicates an entire chapter to this line 'Remember that a person's name is, to that person, the sweetest and most important sound in any language.' It's absolutely true. We love when our name is called (except if it is for a bad reason) in the classroom, in an award ceremony, in a conversation—actually anywhere. The recognition is like music to the listener's ears. So remember to refer to some members of the audience by their names to connect with them better. Modi mentioned Dr Radhakrishnan's name, the Chairman of ISRO and a distinguished alumnus of IIM Bangalore class of 1976.

> I thank the Department of Space, for this opportunity to witness the launch. **I commend Dr K. Radhakrishnan for his leadership.** I wish the team the very best, as you prepare to put our spacecraft into the Mars Orbit, in a few months from now. I wish you every success, as you strive

to master new technologies, and conquer new frontiers of Space. May all your endeavors meet with success!

In the paragraph above, see how wonderfully Modi takes the name of ISRO Chairman and the Department of Space which would be represented by its ministers and officers. And note how he wishes everyone in the audience to do well. All these are excellent ways to connect with your audiences.

3. Outline the shared benefits for the audience. Spell out 'what's in it for them'

The role of the speaker is to meet the objectives he set out before communicating. They can't possibly achieve that without the cooperation of the audience. The audience will not buy the argument easily due to various biases and unexplained mysteries which only they are privy to. So a good practice to overcome this hurdle is to outline the direct and the indirect benefits of your objective to them. I cited the example of Dale Carnegie's book above. If you look at the recent print, you will find '12 things this book will do for you' on the back cover of the book. That is an excellent example of how the author has thought of his audience and connected with them. The topic of the book and the content can turn many people off. But the way the benefits of the book have been outlined for his audience, creates a phenomenal impact. Warren Buffet proudly showcases his certificate of completion of this course in his office. *How to Win Friends and Influence People* has sold 15 million copies since its first print. It only demonstrates how well the book has connected with its audience. Modi does something similar through his speech. Here are some excerpts that highlight the benefits to his audiences—in this case, an entire nation.

Many misunderstand space technology to be for the elite. That it has nothing to do with the common man. **I, however, believe that such technologies are fundamentally connected with the common man.** As a catalyst of change, it can empower and transform lives. Technology opens up new opportunities of development and gives us new ways of addressing our challenges.

Space may seem distant, but is an integral part of our daily life today. It drives our modern communication, connecting even the most remote families to the mainstream. **It empowers the child in the farthest village with quality education, through long-distance learning. It ensures quality healthcare to the most distant person, through Tele-medicine. It enables the youth in a small town with various new job opportunities.** Satellite technology has made distance irrelevant. It effectively enables us to reach the unreached. It helps us connect virtually, where physical connections are difficult.

It has a critical role, in realizing the vision of a Digital India—the power of a connected India.

GIS technology has transformed policy planning, and implementation. Space imaging enables modern management, and conservation of water resources—through GIS-driven watershed development. It has been deployed in our urban planning, to scientifically manage our growing towns and cities. It has also become an important tool, in better managing, and conserving our natural resources. Whether it be the Himalayan glaciers, oceans and forests, coastal resources, or our mineral wealth. **Space imagery is improving our land management systems, bringing wasteland into productive use. Our next frontier, should be to extend the same to land**

> **records, bringing in accuracy and transparency for the common man.**
>
> **Space technology has also evolved into an invaluable asset in disaster management.** Satellite communication channels often end up being the only mode of communication. Accurate advanced warning, and tracking of Cyclone Phailin, saved countless lives recently.

In the paragraphs above, Modi clearly outlines the benefits of the Space Program of India to the entire nation. Once they see the benefits, the audience gets more receptive to your message and hence becomes favourable to making it successful. One of my favourite examples of how a simple idea like this can make things easy is from the movie *Swades*. In the movie, the protagonist Mohan, played by Shah Rukh Khan, goes to visit his foster mother who lives in a remote village in India. He is taken to the Panchayat to greet the elders and they ask him 'What do you do, son?' He responds that 'I work for NASA and we make satellites'; the elders are confused. At this point, his mother intercepts and says, 'Satellites revolve around the earth just like the moon does and tell us when the rains will come. This will help farmers like you to plan the crop accordingly'. Hearing this everybody becomes good-natured. The moment the elders see how Mohan's work in NASA benefits someone like them, they are able to understand the message better. (Swades, 2004)

4. Be humble. Respect the audience

Thanking your audience, mentioning their names, and outlining the benefits are three important and simple ways to connect. Any mechanism where the audience feels respected by the speaker, regardless of the speaker's position is a great way to connect with them. In his first letter to all employees of Microsoft, Satya Nadella said, 'Many companies aspire to change the world. But very few have all the elements required: talent, resources, and perseverance. Microsoft has proven that it has all three in abundance. And as the new CEO, I can't ask for a better foundation. Let's build on this foundation together.' (Nadella, 2014). Respecting your audience's power is a great skill, and if harnessed properly, it can give wonderful results. It requires the speaker to forget one's own credibility for some time and put the audience on a pedestal higher than his own. In many ways, this is what servant leadership is all about. Being humble. A simple rule for this is avoid 'telling' the audience what to do. Rather, show them what you want and invite them to participate. Here is how Modi does it in his speech.

> Development of human resources is critical for our future success. **I was very pleased to meet our young scientists here. I admire their work and their achievements.** Let us link up with more universities and colleges, to develop our future leaders in this area. We must also involve our youth at large, with Space.
>
> You have already started putting a lot of space-related data online, through your Bhuvan space portal. What steps can we take to further increase access to data, by students and researchers? **Let us use social media to further engage with our youth. Let us invite school and college children, to witness launches and visit Space centres. Could we also think of developing, a state-of-the-art, interactive, digital Space Museum?**
>
> In conclusion, I want to emphasize how Technology is central to Development. It touches one and all, and is an important instrument of our national progress.

> **India's Space program is a perfect example of my vision of scale, speed, and skill. Our Space scientists have made us global leaders, in one of the most complex areas of modern technology.** This shows that we can be the best. If we apply ourselves, we can meet the aspirations of our people.

Imagine how powerful these words would be coming from the PM, especially if you were a scientist in that room. I was tracking the story on social media and many of my friends who are usually very vocal against the government and its beaurocracy applauded this speech. I think Modi has brought in a new era of communication in political leadership, instances of which were sorely missing in India. For the first time, a PM recognized his audience, applauded them, and has now invited them to share his vision.

5. Demonstrate cultural sensitivity to your audience

We live in a globalized world and effective communication necessitates that we appreciate the diversity of cultures we encounter. Being sensitive to your audience's socio-cultural concerns is a prerequisite for successful leadership. Gandhi realized that to connect with and lead the people of India, he had to dress like them so they could relate to him. So he decided to wear a simple loin cloth. And by doing so, he created a greater impact than any other leader of India. Many of them like Jinnah, Nehru wore dapper clothes and connected with the elite. But Gandhi became the leader of the masses by looking and living like them. Another brilliant example is Richard Branson in an Indian Maharaja Costume when he launched Virgin Telecom and Virgin Airways in India. These are simple but powerful gestures to connect with your audiences. When I was working for Intel, I went to Japan for the first time to meet my customers. I was supposed to make a presentation of 10 minutes of the new Intel processor that we were working on. I started my talk by bowing down in a Japanese traditional salute and saying 'Oohayu Gozai Mass', which simply means Good Morning in Japanese, and my stock soared with my customers and colleagues out there. I enjoyed eating Sushi and Sashimi with them, appreciated their culture, and they loved me for that. They treated me as one of them. The connection became stronger and many of them are now my good friends. Sushma Swaraj, minister of external relations, covered her head when the Quran was being read at a recent meeting with tourists going to Haj. She even spoke in chaste Urdu. (Swaraj, 2014). Barack Obama would wave at his audiences, acknowledge many of them by a gesture or a sign or even shake hands if they are nearby. Many celebrities spend enormous amounts of time sending personally signed letters as a way to build stronger bonds with their fans. All this makes up the U of the framework.

A QUICK RECAP

Here are nine ways you can win your audiences and connect with them better.

a. Start your speech/message by thanking and acknowledging them
b. Take names. If there is more than one, randomly select a person. Use protocols relevant for the situation. Eg. take name of the senior-most person in the room first and then others depending on the protocol of that country or organization

c. Share the benefits of the topic to your audience. They should get a clear answer to 'what's in it for me'
d. Use 'you' or 'your', 'we' or 'our' sentences more instead of 'I', 'me', or 'mine' sentences
e. Find something common with them like a hobby or activity. It could even be a common school you went to, or a city you have a connection with
f. Say something in their language
g. Dress to suit the occasion and situation
h. Appreciate and respect their culture
i. Greet your audiences by a wave or a sign or a handshake

Let's now go back to the example of Ajay, who has been asked to give a 5 minute update in the next staff meeting to the CEO and his staff. Now let's fill the U box. The simplest way is to thank the CEO and the staff for their valuable time. If you are brave, you can try any one of the other nine techniques mentioned above. I would probably request you to avoid point e or i above as it doesn't suit your position as a young member of the team and would look odd. The most important point here is to highlight how your talk will benefit them with their business goals.

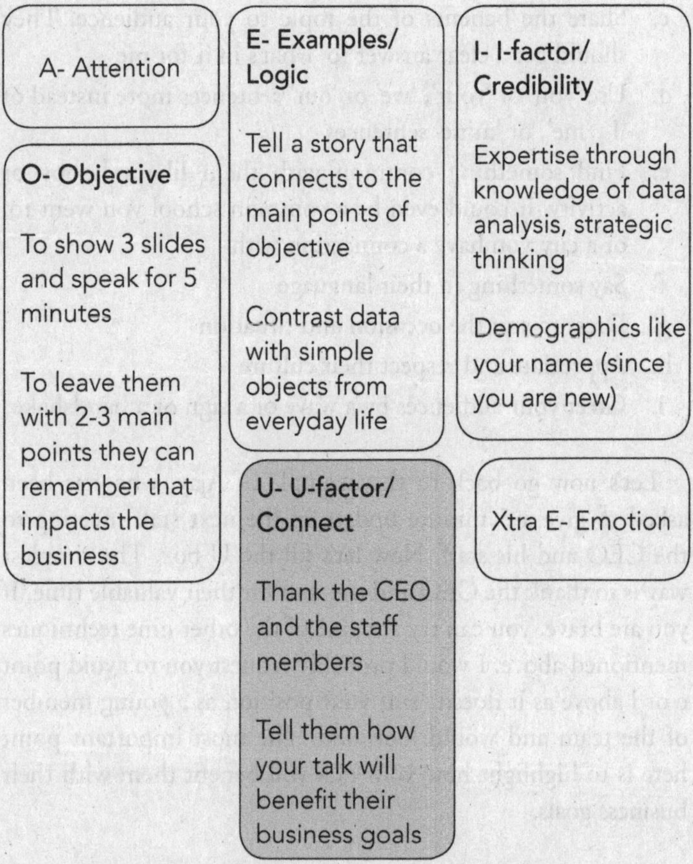

Figure 1: Fill the U of the AEIOU Xtra E framework

EXERCISE

1. What kind of connect do you see in these sentences below. Choose any 1 or more of the 9 techniques to win your audience.

1	Good evening everyone. Thanks a lot for being here.	
2	Bonjour! Kama ta levu?	
3	Your support is critical to the success of this plan.	
4	All of you have made this possible. Great Job. Kudos.	
5	Like you, I am also an engineer and understand the challenges.	
6	Mr Verma worked very hard to make this happen and we are delighted to have him among us.	
7	This is my first visit to your country and I love the food!	
8	Like you, I am also someone's father and someone's child.	
9	Hello Vernita! How is your mother doing? Is she out of the hospital?	
10	I really like that watch you're wearing. Is that Citizen?	

Chapter 9

Keeping the Audience Hooked

In this chapter we will learn how to hook the audience's attention which makes up the A in our framework. Before I move to the next two boxes of the framework, it would be appropriate to take a quick look at where we are. Ajay has filled 4 out of 6 boxes of the framework as depicted in Figure 1. This is not his exact message but just the framework. We will use this framework to make the message in Chapter 11.

If you take a minute to look at the four boxes above, you might now find that we have been able to address some part of the mind of the audience. For a minute, imagine the mind of the audience. I am sure that you would remember diagrams from biology class where the brain looked like a walnut with two distinct halves. The terms left-brain thinker and right-brain thinker are also very popularly used in the corporate world. Roger W. Perry won the Noble Prize in 1981 for this pioneering work which is now used extensively in psychology, medicine, and education. (Perry, 1981). He discovered that the human brain has two very different ways of thinking. The left brain is verbal and analytical. It processes information in a sequential way, looking first at the pieces and then putting it together to get the whole. The right brain is visual and processes information in an intuitive and simultaneous way, looking first at the whole picture then the details.

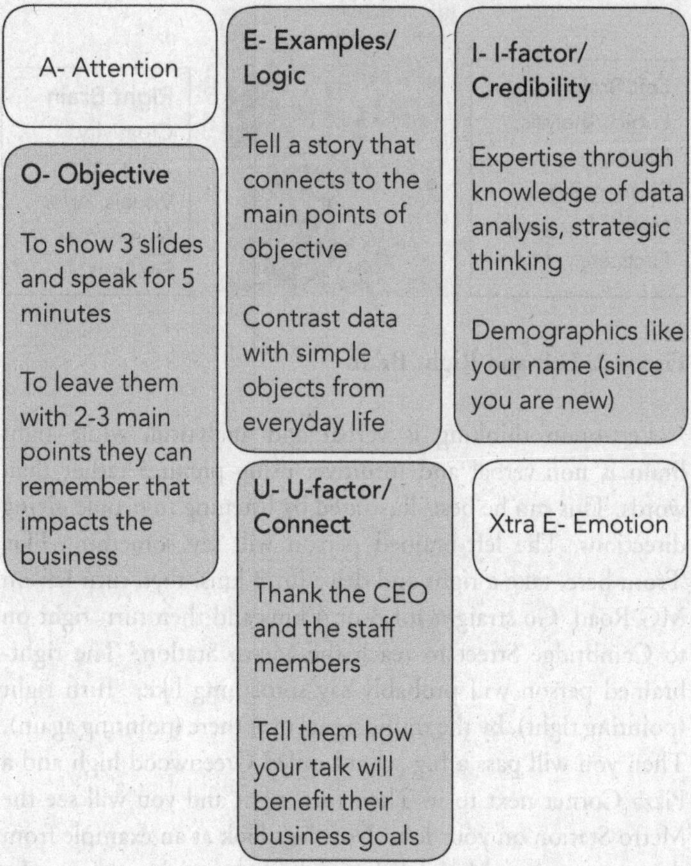

Figure 1: How Ajay's framework looks so far for his presentation

Left Brain
Logic, Analysis,
Linear,
Sequencing,
Maths, Language,
Facts etc

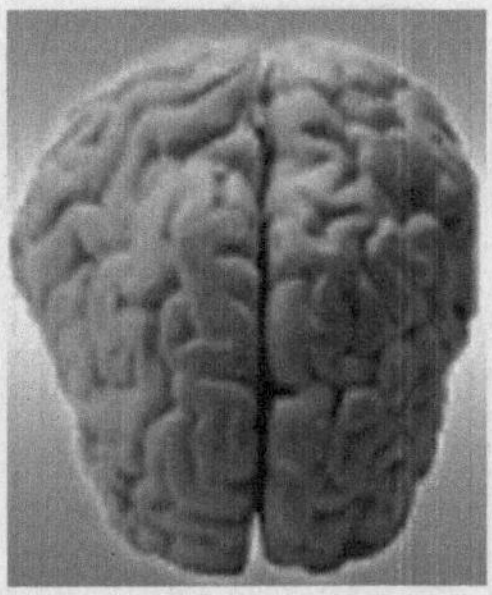

Right Brain
Creativity,
Imagination,
Visuals, Arts,
Non-verbal,
Feelings

Figure 2: Left and Right Brain

Left-brain thinking is verbal and analytical, while right brain is non-verbal and intuitive, using pictures rather than words. This can be best illustrated by listening to people giving directions. The left-brained person will say something like, 'From here, take a right and drive for 3 kms, then turn left on MG Road. Go straight for 3 or 4 kms and then turn right on to Cambridge Street to reach the Metro Station.' The right-brained person will probably say something like, 'Turn right (pointing right), by the traffic signal over there (pointing again). Then you will pass a big school called Greenwood high and a Pizza Corner next to it. Then turn right and you will see the Metro Station on your left.' Now let's look at an example from the corporate world. A left-brained person might explain sales of a beverage like, 'Last year we sold 1.2 billion litres of Pepsi Cola.' A right-brained person might explain the same thing as, 'Last year we sold 1.2 billion litres of Pepsi Cola—that is approximately equal to the water that goes in 48 Olympic size swimming pools'. We discussed ways of making data interesting in Chapter 7. No points in guessing which one of the above will have more impact on the audience. We also use the same kind of approach to teach children. The reading and the mental exercises are taken care of by the left brain and the fun activities are for the right side of the brain. Both these kinds of activities together help a child to learn faster.

The 4 boxes above in figure 1 cater to the left brain of your audience. So how does one cater to the right brain of the audience? Well, we have two boxes to fill still from the 6 above—**Attention and Emotion.** These two will be deployed to serve that objective, as depicted in Figure 3.

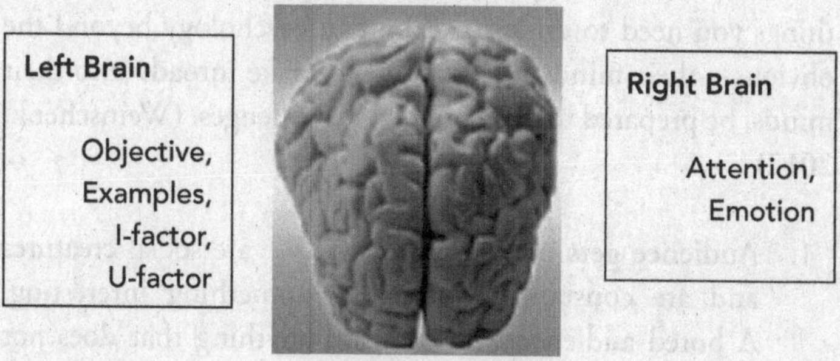

Figure 3: O, E, I and U for left brain and A and Xtra E for right brain

Mathematically, the equation would look something like this

Impact on audience = your message
Impact on audience (left brain + right brain) = AEIOU Xtra E
Left brain = O E C U
Right brain = A Xtra E

The A and Xtra E are like the special ingredients of your message. Without them, the message is less interesting and palatable. With them in the mix, the impact is greater and easier to retain. So as a speaker, always try to formulate your message for the audience in a way that caters to the demands of the right part of the brain too.

In Chapter 2, I had highlighted why communication fails. One major reason is when the speaker fails to understand her audience. There are lots of other factors that can lead to failure which I didn't cover in that chapter. It is time to bring them up. Audiences mostly comprise human beings. There are some basic things you need to understand human psychology beyond the obvious—their minds. If you want to make inroads into their minds, be prepared to overcome these challenges. (Weinschenk, 2012)

1. **Audience gets bored very easily**: We are social creatures and are constantly looking for something interesting. A bored audience will disregard anything that does not pique their interest. They can get bored due to a variety of factors—common ones being stress, overwork, and exhaustion.
2. **Audience has short attention span**: Old scriptures teach us that the greatest power you can possess is the ability to control your own mind. The mind is like an untamed monkey, jumping from one tree to the other. You may get an audience who is not bored to start with. But within a few minutes or even seconds, their minds might jump onto something more interesting. Research done in the 70s and 80s shows that the attention span of a normal human being is about 45 minutes. I bet you, it will be less than 5 minutes now. A research on consumers watching TV or browsing the internet has given some more insights

> and has helped calculate this attention span. It's quite shocking. The attention span of a consumer watching TV or a computer is 5-10 seconds before they lose interest and switch the channel or go to some other website. (Foster, 2014). I am told that the entire TV/Advertising/Media industry uses this fact extensively in their programming. They believe that if the first 30 seconds cannot capture your attention, nothing else will. In general, attention span of audiences has reduced and a key culprit for this are cell phones and other gadgets. Children are the most difficult audiences. Studies show that 1 in 10 children now suffer from a problem called ADHD—Attention deficit hyperactivity disorder that is causing havoc for parents. It is very difficult to get children to focus due to this disorder and it might impact their growth and intelligence. (Rock, 2014)

So what happens when our audience is bored or not interested? Let's take the example of Ajay. He is making his presentation, and talking numbers and facts. Since he is not using our framework, chances are that his talk is very uninteresting and possibly, very soon, the CEO and his staff will start tuning out and checking their emails. End result—he will lose the chance to make his mark and capture the attention. Plus he would have wasted his time and everybody else's. I have highlighted this in the very first chapter where I gave the example of the CEO and his sales VP's never ending and boring speech.

If I draw a graph of the attention span of the audience Ajay is talking to, it might look something like this.

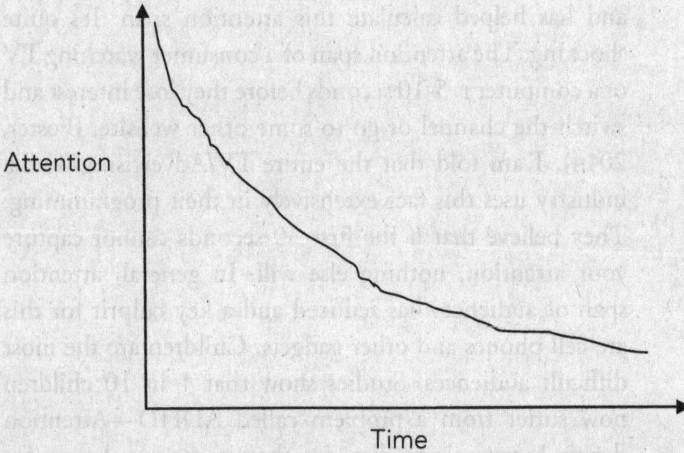

Figure 4: Attention span of audience, if the speaker is not engaging

Ideally the graph should look like this

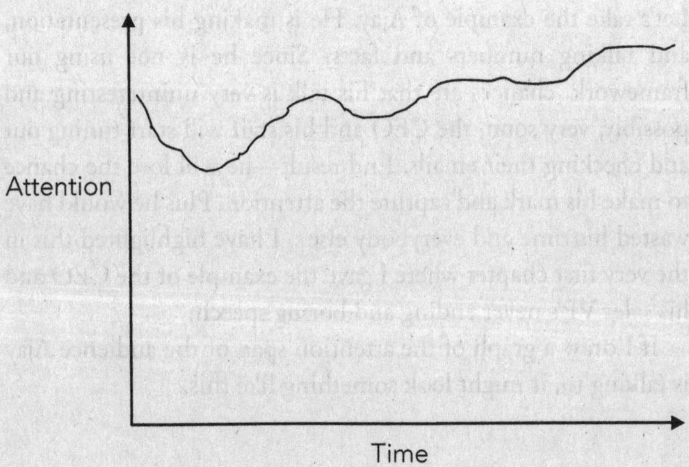

Figure 5: Ideal attention span curve

As a speaker, you should work towards getting the attention span of your audience looking like Figure 5 or better. An attentive audience will be more receptive to your views and hence you might be able to achieve your objectives faster. The best time to capture their attention is at the beginning of the message. They are curious about you and if you can say something that energizes them and grabs their attention, you are on to a great start. You need to ensure that this high level of attention is maintained throughout the talk or else your talk might end up as a disaster. You don't want to be like that movie which starts off looking really promising, but is eventually a dud. Audiences can get very irritated and angry when the movie turns out to be a dud. So watch out.

TECHNIQUES TO ENHANCE AUDIENCE ATTENTION SPAN

As a speaker, you must try and increase the attention span of your audience. Some of the techniques that you could use are listed below. Please note that a critical analysis of the audience present is extremely crucial before you attempt one or more of these. We had discussed how to analyse the audience in Chapter 4 where I spoke about the basic laws of communication.

1. **Hook your audience. Start strong**: Your talk is a performance for your audience. The opening is extremely important. The audience is more attentive and curious in the beginning. So use a powerful hook to start strong. The attention that you capture in the beginning of your talk is very important for the rest of your message. The hook should be relevant to your objective. Some great hooks are
    a. Show a statistic or an interesting fact that is connected to your objective

b. Ask a question connected to the topic and get the audience to respond
c, Tell a story or an anecdote connected to the topic

2. **Smile:** I am certain that you are aware that it takes 72 muscles to frown but only 14 to smile. Enough cheery posters have informed us of this. The importance of smiling is covered in important management articles as well. Bernard Marr, a bestselling author and coach, says that failing to smile can make people uncomfortable, and wonder if you really want to be there. (Marr, 2014). So smile. It's quite easy and gets your audience's attention instantly. There is no law that says that you need to smile only for the first few seconds of your meeting another person. You can choose to keep a pleasant, smiling face throughout the meeting depending on the situation. Many of us are very uncomfortable with smiling. Practise in front of a mirror or a webcam connected to a computer or your phone so that you can become more familiar without feeling silly. A smile is very infectious. The moment you flash it at someone, they mostly tend to smile back. The ice melts and you win their confidence. It also makes your audience comfortable in your presence. Don't assume that you are the only one who is nervous in the room. The audience also has anxiety and it may cause them to be a little cagey or closed. A smile can break through that negativity and warm everyone. Studies indicate that humans tend to be judgmental by nature. The first few seconds do make a lasting impression. The facial expressions are the most important thing that contributes to the first impression. So a smile is one way to make a good first impression. (Willis & Todorov, 2006)

3. **Gestures, body language**

   a. **Come closer to your audience if possible:** This technique can be useful when you are speaking for long durations, typically longer than 15 minutes, and if the room is very large, for instance, a conference room where you are standing near the wall where your presentation is being projected or a classroom where you are facing an entire class. Now only those people who are sitting nearer to you will have high attention. The ones who are sitting farther away from you will have lesser attention. So here is what I do in my classes. After about 5-10 minutes of my talk, I start walking in the room, especially towards those at the back. Then I spend a few minutes at some other place in the room. I personally stick to one place for at least 5 minutes and then naturally walk to some place which I find easy to navigate. If you are presenting with laptops and projectors, and do not have a remote control device, I recommend you stick to the area near the laptop so that it is easy for you manage your slides. It is perfectly okay to stand in one place as well. There is no law that says one has to move. Many speakers stick to their podium stand. It really depends on your style and comfort. And please note, that when you are having a one-on-one conversation, maintain a safe distance from each other. I personally stand at an arm's length—neither too close nor too distant. In many cultures, standing too close can create discomfort for the other person.

   b. **Eye contact:** Eyes are expressive and convey a lot of meanings to the audience. I personally find it very rude when the person I am speaking to does not maintain eye contact. It is also the simplest way to capture attention of your audiences. A bright look will raise their attention span a few notches.

c. **Facial expressions:** When I was a kid, my mother would always find out if I was lying to her. I often asked her how she could make out and she would say, 'Your face gave me the answer'. We may not realize our facial expressions, but the audience makes a lot out of it. A simple frown can convey a message of irritation to your audiences and take your conversation to a very different level. It is always good to maintain a calm and friendly expression on your face.

d. **Hand gestures and body posture:** Our hands and body convey messages too. If we are standing with our hands in our pockets or hugging ourselves tightly, our audiences might get a very different meaning even if we haven't intended it. Over gesticulation can also lead to distractions. So the best is to stand straight, with confidence and use your hands when required to complement your message. I use this technique when I am telling stories or a complicated subject and the hands are very helpful to draw images in the air or to point at something.

4. **Involve the audience:** Audience attention spikes if you ask questions that gives them a chance to participate. They could be as simple as 'What do you think?' or 'Do you agree with this approach?' I have seen several effective leaders also use a quiz to strengthen their talks. Some reward the audience with goodies if get the answers right. Make sure that you give everyone a chance.

5. **Take names**: Nothing gets a person's attention better than calling their name. It is the sweetest sound to a human ear. So feel free to sprinkle your talk with this simple but powerful technique that Dale Carnegie mentioned in his book. (Carnegie, 1936). I usually do this with my back benchers. Works like a charm.
6. **Use of vocal variety**: 'It's not what you say, but how you say that makes the difference.' Our voice is a powerful tool to keep up the engagement of the audience. Any speaker with good voice modulation has a better impact than a speaker who speaks in a monotone. Vocal variety is defined by four parameters.
    a. **Pace**: The speed of your talk. The average speaking speed varies between 120-150 words per minute. Some of us have more and some less. The Guinness record for fastest speaking is 637 words per minute. (Woodmore, 2011). When we are talking to someone in a one-on-one meeting or over phone, we tend to speak fast. In a meeting or a presentation, we have to be slow. Cultures also play a very important role here. Many cultures may not understand your language or accent. So the pace of your talk is very important to maintain the attention of your audience. If you are too fast, you might lose your audience. And if you are too slow, you might bore them. They key is to have the right balance. I personally try to keep my pace at about 100 to 120 words per minute regardless of whether I am teaching or on the phone.
    b. **Tone**: The attitude expressed by your voice. It conveys a feeling to your audience. For example, excitement, happiness, sadness, shock, fears etc. The tone of your voice also helps in blending the right emotion to the

situation of the communication. For instance, if you are congratulating someone, your tone should be enthusiastic. If in a meeting you are talking about the losses that the company has made, your tone should be serious and a bit apologetic.

c. **Volume/pitch**: This is the volume of your voice when you are talking. It can be high, medium, or low and should vary throughout the talk depending on the tone and objective.

d. **Pronunciation/diction/quality**: This is how you speak words. Julian Treasure gave a wonderful TED talk and listed 6 exercises by which you can bring a good vocal variety for your audience. (Treasure, 2013). There are many other resources available on the web to bring in such a variety of tone.

7. **Summarize and transition:** A human mind cannot process more than 7 concepts at a given time. So if you have to talk about multiple concepts, a good technique to help the audience assimilate and retain is by summarizing it before moving on to the next one. A sentence that is commonly used is 'Here is what I have told you so far. Here is what I am going to talk next'. Another way to do this is, 'Let's step back for a minute and look at what we have discussed so far.' This way, the audience also transitions smoothly from one point to the other and the flow is maintained.
8. **Pause:** As the audience is listening to the speaker's words, their minds start to process the message simultaneously. A pause in the speech or presentation ensures that they get time to digest the message better. It should ideally be a gap of 1-2 seconds between few sentences or a paragraph. An

effective pause also enhances the impact of the talk. The key here is to pause at the right time. A speaker should deliver his message in a series of bursts with appropriate pauses—like dashes and dots in a Morse code.

A QUICK RECAP

Here are five ways you can keep your audiences engaged in your talk.

1. Hook your audiences in the opening part of your message. Start strong
2. Use your voice and the vocal variety through volume, tone, diction, and speed
3. Use body language as appropriate—hands, movements, facial expressions, smile, eyes
4, Pause appropriately. Give the audience time to digest what has been conveyed
5. Summarize and transition between key points so that the flow of the talk is smooth

Let's now go back to Ajay's framework. And now let's fill the A (attention) box. A great opening is most desirable as it ensures attention for a longer time. And vocal variety would make the speech more interesting. Breaks or pauses, will help the audience process your points and retain them longer, and a smooth transition from concept A to B will help them understand the logical flow better.

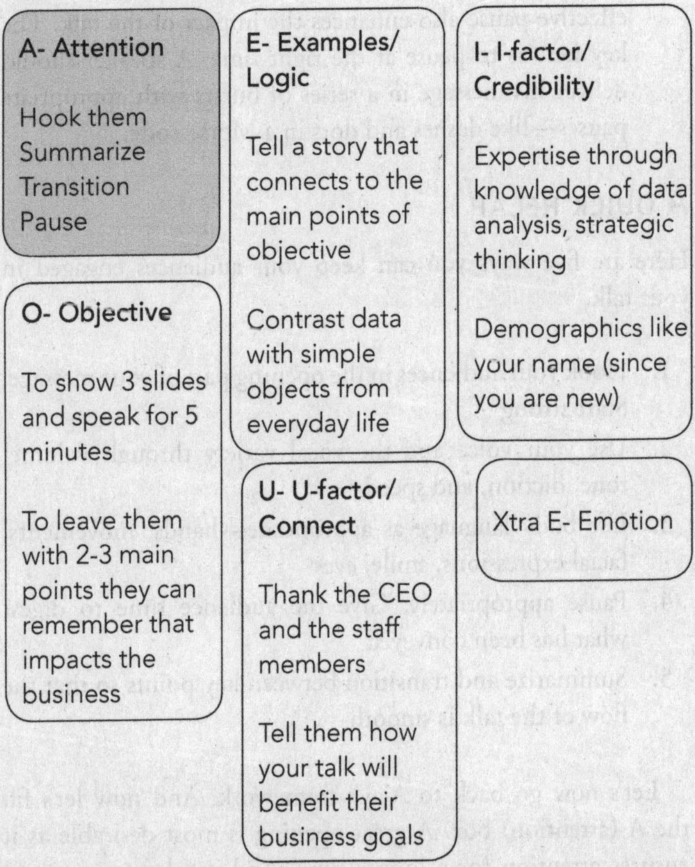

Figure 6: Filling the Attention box for the framework

Exercise

1. You work for a mobile application company and are in the 3GSM conference. You are walking and chance to see a top CEO of a mobile handset company. He is very difficult to get and you are very keen to have a tie-up with his company so that they can pre-load your application in their phones. How will you approach him and capture his attention so that he doesn't forget you?
2. You are in a meeting and giving a talk. You notice that everyone is checking their phones and are distracted. What will you do to bring the attention back to your talk?

Chapter 10

Emotions: The Secret Sauce

We covered the Attention box in the last chapter. In this chapter, we will focus on emotions which make up the Xtra E of our framework. This is a very important ingredient in your message and has the ability to drown out all other inadequacies if used effectively. Great orators and statesmen like Atal Bihari Vajpayee, Abraham Lincoln, and Winston Churchill have used this brilliantly to evoke the desired responses in their audience. Hitler, despicable though his propaganda might have been, used this most effectively. Call it the salt or sugar of the dish. A good communicator will sprinkle just the right amount of emotion in her speech. It should be as per taste. Too much and it could spoil the dish. Too little and the dish might be insipid or tasteless. It is imperative to get this just right.

Before we understand how to use this box in our framework, let me first explain how we experience emotions in our everyday life. Emotions are all around us. Here are some scenarios from my own life that make me experience few emotions everyday.

1. When I wake up in the morning and see my children and my wife sleeping cozily in their blankets. I feel a **warm feeling of security and love.**
2. I am late for the day already and my daughter who is not finishing her glass of milk is delaying me further as I have to drop her to school first. I experience **irritation and anger.**

3. While driving, I am stopped at a signal by a policeman for no fault of mine. I am fined and I feel **helpless, angry, and frustrated.**
4. Back inside a car, the RJ plays my favorite songs and I feel **happy** again.
5. At work, I have a deadline to catch up and really don't want anybody to bother me. At that moment, a colleague steps in and wants to chat. I feel **irritated** and am **afraid** that I will miss my deadline and lose my customer.
6. By afternoon, mental **fatigue** sets in and a cup of coffee **refreshes** me.
7. By evening I am ready to stop and go back home. I feel **happy** again.
8. Sleep **relaxes** me.

Indian scriptures and dance forms describe nine emotions—the Navrasa. They are

1. Love
2. Joy
3. Wonder
4. Peace
5. Anger
6. Courage
7. Sadness
8. Fear
9. Disgust

In my list of emotions I felt above, I felt 5 out of 9 navrasas. Each day is different. If I consider myself—the days I experience more positive emotions is also a very productive day for me. And if someone in office is in a bad mood, it does impact me and hence my family when I go back home. It's called the Contagion of Emotions and has been proven to affect the people in the social networks like Facebook and Twitter. You spread your emotions in a room full of people too—doesn't matter if the room is the internet or a physical, walled room. (Adam D. I. Kramer, 2014). So if your words convey something to your audiences and make them feel an emotion, you can trigger a contagion that can spread powerfully forward.

Why are Emotions Important for Communication

1. **Emotions help your audiences in making decisions:** The entire marketing machinery of an organization will use every weapon in their armoury to trigger the emotions in you. They will appeal to your emotions that buying a black soda water in a glass bottle will quench your thirst, make you look super cool, help the Indo-Pak dosti project, save the environment, and if that doesn't nail your 'yes', they will dangle in front of you a date with Deepika Padukone. And guess what—sales rocket up and there are SMSs of codes from caps of bottles flying around. Why? Because you were emotionally pulled into making this decision. My wife and children have perfected certain emotional blackmailing techniques to get what they want from me. There is ample evidence to prove that emotions help in making decisions. (Bechara, 2004). And a book called *Buyology* can dispel every myth on how smart advertising and marketing professionals are actually making you buy things by manipulating your emotions. If you watch an ad of someone eating the KFC burger and licking his or her fingers provocatively, chances are it might trigger you to buy a KFC burger very soon. The ad manipulates your emotions and makes you crave the burger. Sometimes,

the decision is just irrational. But that is the whole point he tried to make in the book—that your decisions are controlled by some smart marketing person in KFC. (Lindstorm, 2008) (Martino, 2006)

2. **They are universally accepted**: Paul Ekman, who studied human emotions, discovered six facial expressions that almost everyone recognizes worldwide. These are happiness, sadness, anger, fear, disgust, and surprise. These basic emotions are accepted and understood by people all over the world, and can be used to communicate. (Ekman, 2003)
3. **We process and understand expressions before logic**: The brain is a complex machine. Imagine it to be a factory where things are done in sequence. In this factory, emotions are processed faster and quicker. Logic takes much longer to process. This is the reason stories are more impactful in communication because they convey emotions; and emotions are processed faster. A smile from you to your audience will get processed faster than the first sentence you utter. If you recall the biology classes, you will remember that the signals come to our brain from our sensory organs. They all enter our brain through a common entry point just above our neck and then spread out to 3 areas. The first entry point of the brain is called the Reptilian brain. It processes basic emotions like fear and love and basic survival instincts of life. The signals then enter the second part of the brain called the Limbic brain where we have our memories and behaviour traits. Then the signals travel to the last part of our brain which is the most advanced and also the reason we are different from animals—its called the NeoCortex. That is where the brains starts to process logic and takes a decision based on intelligence. This entire theory was first postulated by

Dr Paul Maclean and is called the Triune brain theory. The key message that I want to leave you with from this theory is that brains process emotions faster than logic. So if your messages have emotional qualities, it might create more impact on your audiences. (Maclean, 1960)

4. **Emotion are the loop holes to your audience's fortresses:** As we see in the point 1, 2 and 3 above, the best way to get to your audiences is through emotions. If you remember the famous battle of Troy, the Greek armies tried their best to conquer Troy. But the fort was impregnable and the Trojans put up a brave fight. So the Greeks came up with an ingenious plan. They made a huge wooden horse which was hollow from inside. Some of the best Greek soliders hid in it. And the remaining pretended to sail away. When the Trojans saw the Greeks retreating, and saw a huge wooden horse outside, they thought that it was a victory trophy and brought it inside the fortress to celebrate their victory. Once the horse was brought inside, the Greek soldiers came out, opened the gate to the other Greeks who had secretly sailed back, stormed the fortress and defeated the Trojans. So the Trojan Horse was the loophole to get into the fortress. Emotions are similar loop holes. They are very difficult to find, but once you do, you can win your audiences easily.

An analysis of J.K. Rowling's speech at Harvard

J.K. Rowling delivered the Harvard Commencement Address in 2008. I knew that she was a great writer because I loved reading all the seven Harry Potter books; but another of her talents presented itself during her 20 minute talk. I was floored by her views and the thoughts she conveyed in her speech to the

Harvard students. I went through an emotional roller coaster myself. She made people laugh, think, and feel a variety of emotions like humour, wonder, joy, fear, and finally hope and exaltation. Here are few sentences in a table where I highlight the emotions.

Emotion	Sentence
Humour/Wit	Not only has Harvard given me an extraordinary honour, but the weeks of fear and nausea I have endured at the thought of giving this commencement address have made me lose weight. A win-win situation! Now all I have to do is take deep breaths, squint at the red banners and convince myself that I am at the world's largest Gryffindor reunion.
Sarcasm	Delivering a commencement address is a great responsibility; or so I thought until I cast my mind back to my own graduation. The commencement speaker that day was the distinguished British philosopher Baroness Mary Warnock. Reflecting on her speech has helped me enormously in writing this one, because it turns out that I can't remember a single word she said. This liberating discovery enables me to proceed without any fear that I might inadvertently influence you to abandon promising careers in business, the law or politics for the giddy delights of becoming a gay wizard. You see? If all you remember in years to come is the 'gay wizard' joke, I've come out ahead of Baroness Mary Warnock. Achievable goals: the first step to self improvement.

Hope-lessness	That period of my life was a dark one, and I had no idea that there was going to be what the press has since represented as a kind of fairy tale resolution. I had no idea then how far the tunnel extended, and for a long time, any light at the end of it was a hope rather than a reality.
Pity	There in my little office I read hastily scribbled letters smuggled out of totalitarian regimes by men and women who were risking imprisonment to inform the outside world of what was happening to them. I saw photographs of those who had disappeared without trace, sent to Amnesty by their desperate families and friends. I read the testimony of torture victims and saw pictures of their injuries. I opened handwritten, eye-witness accounts of summary trials and executions, of kidnappings and rapes.
Horror	And as long as I live I shall remember walking along an empty corridor and suddenly hearing, from behind a closed door, a scream of pain and horror such as I have never heard since. The door opened, and the researcher poked out her head and told me to run and make a hot drink for the young man sitting with her. She had just had to give him the news that in retaliation for his own outspokenness against his country's regime, his mother had been seized and executed.

Provoke	But how much more are you, Harvard graduates of 2008, likely to touch other people's lives? Your intelligence, your capacity for hard work, the education you have earned and received, give you unique status, and unique responsibilities. Even your nationality sets you apart. The great majority of you belong to the world's only remaining superpower. The way you vote, the way you live, the way you protest, the pressure you bring to bear on your government, has an impact way beyond your borders. That is your privilege, and your burden.
Hope/Joy	I have one last hope for you, which is something that I already had at 21. The friends with whom I sat on graduation day have been my friends for life. They are my children's godparents, the people to whom I've been able to turn in times of trouble, people who have been kind enough not to sue me when I took their names for Death Eaters. At our graduation we were bound by enormous affection, by our shared experience of a time that could never come again, and, of course, by the knowledge that we held certain photographic evidence that would be exceptionally valuable if any of us ran for Prime Minister. So today, I wish you nothing better than similar friendships. And tomorrow, I hope that even if you remember not a single word of mine, you remember those of Seneca,

	another of those old Romans I met when I fled down the Classics corridor, in retreat from career ladders, in search of ancient wisdom: 'As is a tale, so is life: not how long it is, but how good it is, is what matters.' I wish you all very good lives.

Table 1: Emotions in Rowling's speech

If I remember correctly, the audience clapped and laughed more than five times in those 20 minutes before giving her a standing ovation. Her words really moved the audience to stand up. She used the universal power of emotions to create Harry Potter and use the same principals in her speech. Harry Potter is now all over the world. He lives in the hearts of children regardless of the fact whether they are born in India, China, UK, USA, or Africa. He is a reluctant hero, one which every child can relate to; and his story is one of love, loyalty, and ultimate triumph of good over evil. It is a magic that transcends geographical and cultural boundaries.

Techniques to Trigger Desired Emotions in Your Audience

So how does one bring out the desired emotions in an audience? We have discussed few such techniques in earlier chapters. We will outline all of them again now.

1. **Storytelling:** In the speech from Rowling earlier, when she tells the story of the man from Africa, you can visualize the man right in front of your eyes with Rowling holding his hand and walking towards the train. Stories have the

ability to touch hearts and speak to you. They paint vivid pictures in our minds and move us. We have discussed this topic at length in Chapter 9 and also in earlier in this chapter about how storytelling has to be combined with an appropriate vocal variety to convey a message better.

2. **Humour:** This is one of the most underutilized techniques during communication. It seems we have forgotten to have fun. Seriousness and lack of time have compounded the early demise of fun at work and in our lives. We make boring presentations because we think that fun might not be taken in the right spirit by your audiences especially in the corporate circles.. Rowling cracks 2-3 witty jokes in her speech and regales her audiences. And notice how she used the technique of 'hook' that we discussed in Chapter 9 in the first paragraph of her talk. Her hook was self-deprecating joke; and it had a lightening effect on her audience. It warmed them, made the atmosphere more relaxed, and at the same time ensured the attention of her audience.
3. **Provocation:** This technique is used in talks where the speaker has a very opinionated stand on a topic. You ask hard hitting questions to your audiences and provoke them to think. The emotions help them decide and act. In her famous speech, a small young school girl from Canada, Severn Suzuki threw very hard hitting and thought-provoking questions at the UN Earth Summit Rio in 1992. Here are some examples from her speech.
    a. *I am afraid to go out in the sun now because of the holes in the ozone. I am afraid to breathe the air because I don't know what chemicals are in it. Did you have to worry about these little things when you were my age?*
    b. *At school, even in kindergarten, you teach us to behave in the world. You teach us:*

Not to fight with others, to work things out, to respect others, to clean up our mess, not to hurt other creatures to share—not be greedy.

Then why do you go out and do the things you tell us not to do?

c. *Do not forget why you're attending these conferences, who you're doing this for—we are your own children. You are deciding what kind of world we will grow up in.*

d. *Well, what you do makes me cry at night. You grown ups say you love us. I challenge you, please make your actions reflect your words.*

These questions emerged like bullets and hit the spot—forcing the audience to think. The video also has footage of the people listening to her and you can make out from their gestures and expressions that they were shaken out of their comfort zone. (Suzuki, 1992)

4. **Arguments:** Nothing can beat facts, data, and logical arguments to bring out emotions in your audiences. Edwards Deming, a well-known author and scholar, said, 'Without data, you are just another person with an opinion.' If the logic of the argument is weak, your audiences cannot be convinced to act favourably. Parliamentary debates are a great source to watch how statesmen and leaders change public opinion. A great movie to see is *12 Angry Men* or its Hindi equivalent *Ek Ruka Hua Faisla*. (Lumet, 1957). The movie starts with a very simple plot. There are 12 jury members who are supposed to decide the fate of a young boy who has been accused of killing his own father. The evidence points at the convict being guilty. 11 out of 12 vote yes but 1 gentleman provides arguments that slowly turn everyone's conviction. Emotions play a very crucial role in this as seen by the brilliant performances by all actors of the movie.

Sushma Swaraj's scathing attack on prices of essentials to the Finance Minister Pranab Mukherjee in 2011 is a wonderful example of how a speaker uses facts and figures to change the opinion through emotions. At that time Pranab Mukherjee was the finance minister and would have probably mentioned that the economy and inflation were under control. Sushma Swaraj stood and talked about the price of common essentials that she bought for her own house and how her data showed that prices were way above what the finance minister had quoted. Her emotional pitch was very convincing as she brought the story of a common housewife and her dilemma into the inflation situation of the country. (Swaraj, 2011). We have dedicated an entire chapter on this earlier. The point to remember here is to combine argument with vocal variety to bring emotions in the audiences.

A QUICK RECAP

Emotions are important because of the following four reasons

a. Emotions help your audiences in making decisions
b. They are universally accepted
c. They are the expressions we process and understand first before logic
d. They are the loop holes to your audiences fortresses

Here are four ways you can bring emotions in your audiences

a. Storytelling
b. Humour
c. Provocation
d. Arguments

Let's now take the example of Ajay's framework for his presentation. In the previous chapter, we used the AEIOU Xtra E framework and completed the A box. Now let's fill the last box called Xtra E. The simplest emotion one can give is that of joy, empathy through a simple courteous greeting and joy. Then one can give an emotion of wonder by an interesting fact nicely presented using the techniques we spoke about earlier and leave your CEO and his staff with, 'Wow! I didn't know that' and you are done.

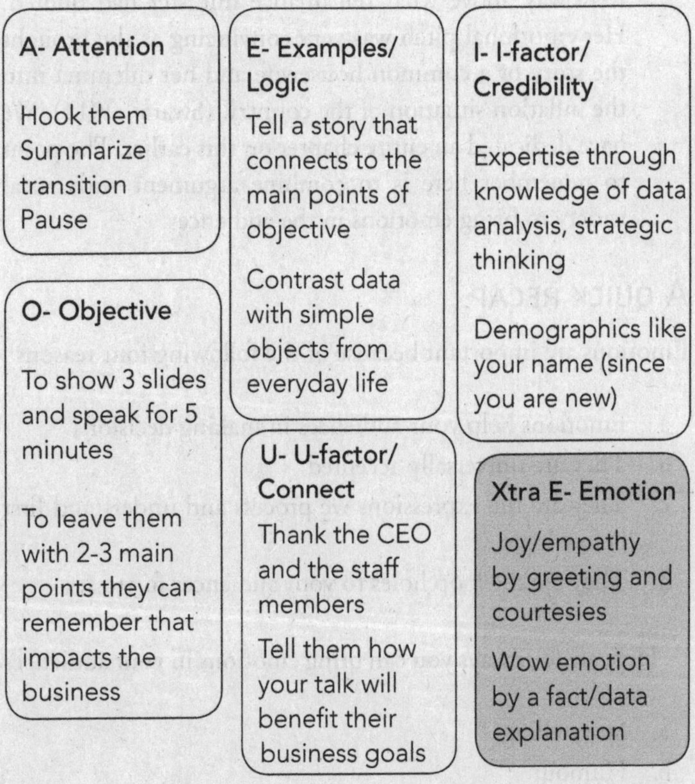

Figure 1: The Xtra E box of the framework

EXERCISE

1. Imagine you are giving a farewell party to your colleague who reported to you but has decided to leave your company for a better opportunity. What emotions will you sprinkle in your farewell speech and how?
2. You are interviewing a candidate for a job in your team.
   a. What would you do and say so that he feels comfortable with you?
   b. What would you say so that he is happy with the interview?
   c. What would you do to end the interview and make this person feel great about the whole experience?
3. You are on the phone with a very angry customer. He bought your product—a laptop—but found out that it is faulty. You found out that the fault is not really yours but because of a third party printer which is causing the problem. What would you avoid telling this customer which arouses further anger and frustration in him.

CHAPTER 11

Putting the Message Together

LET'S ENCAPSULATE WHAT AJAY HAS done so far for his presentation. He has gone through the elements of persuasive message and has come up with a basic framework by filling the 6 boxes of the AEIOU and Xtra E framework. Now let us help him in putting this all together and creating an actual message.

THE SIZE OF THE MESSAGE

An important aspect of communication is the size of the message. If it is too long, the audience loses attention. If it is too short, it might not convey the intent. The size of the message has to be just right for the audiences. And it is a very difficult thing to achieve. It's called 'brevity'. Brevity is not about writing or speaking less, it's about succinctly communicating your points. Twitter was the first medium to define an upper limit to the size of a message—140 characters, and give a measurement to brevity. There are many examples on how messages on Twitter reached the audiences faster than any medium and created a huge impact. The Arab Spring revolution of January 2011 that spread in Egypt, Tunisia, and Libya are also called Twitter revolutions. The good old telegram system was based on a similar principle, but there was no upper limit. The greater the length of the message, the more one had to pay to transmit it.

So brevity was important to keep the cost of communication low. An average human speaks roughly 150 words a minute. So using that calculation, Ajay can speak a maximum of 150*5 = 750 words in the time allotted to him. If you anticipate questions from the audience, you should factor in 1 or 2 minutes for those. So, if you take a minute out for questions, you now have 4 minutes, i.e., 150*4 = 600 words tops. Since Ajay has to make a presentation, it might be a good idea to have him make some slides to complement his talk. A good thumb rule for the number of slides is Time/2. So our friend should make maximum 2 slides for the 4 minute slot. Here is a simple table to remember this better

Size of the message (verbal)	(Time allotted–time for Q&A) * 150 words
Number of slides (presentation)	(Time allotted –time for Q&A)/ 2 slides

Table 1: Size of the message

STRUCTURE OF THE MESSAGE

A message has a beginning, a middle, and an end. Some also call it the opening, body, and conclusion. It is a structure that is universally accepted and widely used. As a master chef of your message, you can follow a recipe which I mention here, but feel free to improvise with your own creativity as well.

The Opening

The simplest purpose of an opening is to inform your audiences—I am so and so and I am going to tell you this. Besides this objective, you can also use the opening to gain the attention of your audience. So the boxes from the framework that you may want to use here are I, A, and O—I-factor or credibility, Attention, and Objective. You could avoid using the I-factor box if the audience knows who you are already.

The Body

Once you have outlined the objective of your message to the audience, it is time to tell them the message properly so that they can understand it better. The boxes from the framework that you should use here are E, I, U, and Xtra E—examples or logic, I-factor or credibility, U-factor or connect, and emotion.

The Conclusion

Once you have communicated your message, summarize what you have told them. Re-emphasize your objective to ensure that you meet your purpose.

What I mentioned above is not the gold standard. You are free to mix and match depending on your audiences and the objective. After all, creativity knows no bounds. It's important that you improvise on this framework to suit your and your audience's needs. So now we are ready to draft our message.

A- Attention

Hook them
Summarize
transition
Pause

O- Objective

To show 3 slides and speak for 5 minutes

To leave them with 2-3 main points they can remember that impacts the business

E- Examples/ Logic

Tell a story that connects to the main points of objective

Contrast data with simple objects from everyday life

U- U-factor/ Connect

Thank the CEO and the staff members

Tell them how your talk will benefit their business goals

I- I-factor/ Credibility

Expertise through knowledge of data analysis, strategic thinking

Demographics like your name (since you are new)

Xtra E- Emotion

Joy/empathy by greeting and courtesies

Wow emotion by a fact/data explanation

Figure 1: The complete AEIOU Xtra E Framework

Drafting the Message

By looking at Figure 1 above, let's draft our message by using a simple table.

Opening	Attention	Good morning to all of you (with an energetic enthusiastic tone)
	Credibility	My name is Ajay and I have joined as a graduate management trainee from IIM Bangalore
	Objective	In the next 4 minutes, I will give you a quick analysis of the businesses based on the data shared with me 2 weeks ago. My intention is to help you with insights that can help in strategic decisions and make your businesses more profitable. I will answer questions you might have in the end
Body	Connect	Like Mr Amit mentioned in his talk before me, our goal is to improve our shareholder's value. I believe like all of you in this room that we have a tremendous opportunity in front of us.
	Examples	Last week, my mother ordered some hair care products from the local department store. The shopkeeper didn't have our brands and my mother took our competitor brands instead. I looked at our figures. In Jaipur, where my parents live, we are #4 in the product category and I was shocked because we are #1 and #2 everywhere else in India. I have 2 more interesting facts to share with you. One is that despite our strong brand recall in Jaipur, thanks to the good ad push by Mr Rajiv's team,

		our channels barely push our product into the market. The competition incentivizes them more than us and if we could match them or make it better, we will increase our sales by 40 percent. And Lastly, the recent budget has given us a good opportunity to increase local production by tax benefits. So your teams can now make more margins.
	Credibility	So coming back to the problem in Jaipur, I dug further into the data by using a technique called gap analysis that I learnt in my marketing course at B school and found that all we need is a little push in our distribution channels on our product. There is no extra cost of doing this as we already have a budget which is unutilized.
	Xtra Emotion	We will become #2 and #1 soon in Jaipur and my mom will not have to buy our competitor's products anymore.
Conclusion	Attention	In summary, I want to mention that in Jaipur we can do a lot better by little incentives to the distribution channels.
	Objective	This will increase sales and our overall objective.
	Connect	I thank all of you for this wonderful opportunity and If you have any questions, I will be happy to answer them now.

Table 2: Drafting the message using the framework

So as you can see, we have a basic message with all elements of the framework visible. Now as a chef of this message, you can sprinkle more emotion, examples, and connect as per your objective, comfort, and audience. We just wrote 385 words and there is room for about 200 more. A good communicator will make at least 2-3 drafts before it is ready to be presented. Some speakers even make 10 drafts. The speechwriter of Barack Obama, Jon Favreau gave a talk at the Harvard Law school and explained how Obama and he would revise his speeches multiple times. And we all know how impactful those speeches are. Sometimes, you may have to trash the entire message and start all over again. (Favreau, 2013)

Polishing your prose

Once your script is ready, you need to polish it till it gleams. Consider yourself an artist or a chef. As a chef, once your dish is prepared, you need to plate it. Plating is an art in itself and the presentation of your dish can make or break the culinary experience for the person. Similarly, you can use a technique called 'polishing your prose' to make your talk more effective. (Steven Cahn, 2013). There are three steps to do this.

1. **Eliminate duplicate and unnecessary words:** Let us take a sentence from the script above 'In the next 4 minutes, I will give you a quick analysis….', the meaning and impact of the sentence remains exactly the same if I drop the first 5 words 'In the next 4 minutes'. You are really not going to be measured on a stop watch by anyone except you. So they don't need to know. Scrub your entire script and delete words like these.
2. **Shorten sentences**: An effective speaker will speak short sentences—no more than 15 words per sentence. Try

and break your sentences if they are long. It helps the audiences to follow your message properly. An example is the sentence from the script above 'So coming back to the problem in Jaipur, I dug into the data more using a technique called gap analysis that I learnt in my marketing course at B school and found that all we need is a little push in our distribution channels on our product'. It is 47 words. We should try and break it into 3-4 sentences. Here we go—*So coming back to the problem in Jaipur, I dug into the data. I used a technique called gap analysis that I learnt in my marketing course at B school. I found that all we need is a little push in our distribution channels on our product.*

3. **Rephrase sentences to make them more impactful:** Many times, we can rephrase our sentences to make them sound and read better. For example, if I take the three sentences from point number 2 above, we can rephrase them as—*I analysed the sales data from Jaipur using gap analysis technique from my marketing course. All we need is a little push in our distribution channels on our product.* So from a long sentence of 47 words, we first broke down the sentence to 3 and then rephrased it to make it 2 sentences of 27 words in all. We almost reduced our prose by 40 percent.

This technique is very powerful and once mastered can do wonders to your messages—both spoken and written. Many times, you may not have the time or luxury to do a written analysis. But with regular practice, your mental skills should internalize this technique for every message that you speak even if it is impromptu. Steven Cahn and Victor Cahn have written a wonderful book called *Polishing your Prose* which can help you and is a great example of how this works is on a website that is publicly accessible. (Cahn & Cahn, 2013)

VISUALS AND SLIDES

Once your speech is ready, you should now prepare some slides that can aid your talk. They also help in capturing the audience's attention and emotions. A good visual appeals to the right brain of your audience. I won't spend too much time on this because that is not the focus of this book. But I would like to give some pointers to do this step right.

a. **A picture is worth a thousand words** – your slides should complement your script. Since your script has rich words, examples, and stories, accompany them with a slide which is visually appealing for your audience. E.g. a visual like a picture or a diagram or a chart that is relevant for the words you will be speaking at that time.
b. **Use bigger fonts** – many people in the audience may not be able to read the content in your slides if they are sitting at the back of the room. Ensure that you choose bigger fonts so that everyone can read them easily.
c. **Use call outs** – if you have a complicated visual, use call outs or point to an area where you want the audience to focus on with an appropriate message. Call outs are like pointers towards a certain area of the visual in the slide and emphasize the message. If you look at all print ads from top companies, they plan the print in such a way that your eyes will focus on the area that gives them maximum mileage. In a campaign done by Colgate toothpaste, the audience notice specks of food in the teeth but not the physical defects of the people in that ad. The message of the ad was 'food caught on your teeth gets more attention than any physical defect'. (Dayley, 2013). So if you don't direct the focus of your audience to a particular area of your visual, they will look elsewhere and lose attention.

Once they lose attention, they cannot concentrate to your words and the impact is lost.

d. **Let the audience absorb the visual** – an audience finds it very difficult to absorb a visual and process your words simultaneously. So put the visual, give them a moment to look at it, and then slowly start speaking to explain what the slide conveys. Or speak about it first and then put the visual at the right time to complement your words. The animation techniques in softwares like PowerPoint and Prezzy are good resources to build your slides with.

e. **Check the AV equipment/software compatibility** – In one of the talks I had with a customer, I was using a software version which was different than the one on the computer at the customer place. So when I loaded my slides on that computer, the fonts went haywire. The video stopped playing and the audience lost attention. All I needed to ensure was to check the equipment and compatibility of the software 15 minutes before my talk. Sometimes, these minor glitches are unpardonable mistakes as they cause huge problems.

DELIVERING THE MESSAGE

You are now ready to deliver or transmit your message. This is the time you should decide what medium to choose—phone call, face-to-face meeting, email, letter, etc. Every medium has its pros and cons. A personal face-to-face meeting is most desirable but not always possible. Phone calls have become very important and easy mechanisms. Emails and other written forms require a lot more effort, and also have delayed impact. The only request I have for you at this point is this—ask yourself, do you really have to send the message. If the answer is yes, go ahead. Otherwise, Shut Up!

EXERCISES

1. List down 2 or 3 situations where you should shut up.
2. You are a project manager and things are getting delayed. You need to inform your customer about the bad news. What medium will you choose—a phone call or an email and why?
3. In the example above, lets say you chose an email. How many words will you write (maximum)? Plot the AEIOU Xtra E framework.
4. You work for Mckinsey and have a very demanding client. You have prepared a 600 page report and 100 slides which cover the entire project findings and recommendations. But you are supposed to present your entire recommendations to the client's leadership team in 20 minutes out of which 10 minutes will be Q&A. How will you design your slides so that you convey your recommendations?

Part 3

CHAPTER 12

Communication in the Business Context

COMMUNICATION IS AN ALL-PERVASIVE TOPIC. We are social beings by nature and communication is the underlying fabric of our interaction with other social beings. We now move into the last part of the book which focuses on how to apply the AEIOU Xtra E framework in various scenarios that we encounter in our daily lives.

We spend more than half of our life in an office. There are various scenarios where we should know what to say and when to shut up. In this chapter, I will take the most common scenarios where we can use this framework and make our impact to our audiences. They are as follows

1. Making a presentation—we already covered this in the last 6 chapters with the example of Ajay who was to make a presentation to the CEO and his staff
2. Handling job interviews (with you as the applicant)
3. Communication in a conflict—how does one resolve a conflict with colleagues and customers
4. Giving and receiving feedback
5. Communicating in a difficult situation
6. Saying No
7. Saying sorry

Handling job interviews

A job interview is a very important communication scenario in our lives and the AEIOU Xtra E framework can be of immense help to you. Interviewing is a very biased activity where the interviewer is trying to fit you into the role she is interviewing you for. An organization is like a big machine where each employee fits in a specific role. Each role has a specification. An interview is a well-known process that tests how you fit into that role. The interviewer tests the candidate by asking various questions to which the candidate has to respond to the best of their ability. This is where our AEIOU Xtra E framework can be very helpful to candidates attending the job interview.

The interviewer is like the audience of this communication process. Just like how we discussed in the earlier chapters, the candidate must understand and analyse his audience to prepare a persuasive message. So what does the interviewer expect from the candidate? I think all that the interviewer wants from the candidate's answers is how he will adopt to the role and the company. The interviewer's mind has similar halves—one is logical and one is creative. Just as we discussed earlier, the audience has the following questions in their mind as listed under.

1. Who are you
2. What do you want from me
3. Why should I agree with you/Prove your point (Convince me)
4. What's in it for me

These questions above change slightly for the job interviewer as below

1. Tell me something about yourself
2. Why should I hire you
3. Give me some examples of your accomplishments, skills and personality that suit this role
4. What benefit will you bring to the company

Now, these questions are mostly going to satisfy the left side of the brain of the interviewer. From our AEIOU Xtra E framework, you have 4 boxes that satisfy the 4 questions above. Don't forget the right brain and the power of creativity to make an impact. The right brain of the interviewer is expecting something that makes you more interesting. And you have 2 boxes from the framework to help you with that. The figure below helps explain this better.

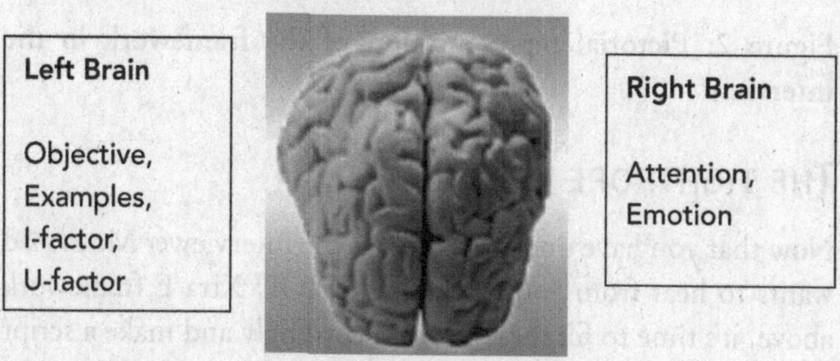

Figure 1: The framework in a job interview

So assume we have a candidate called Neha and she has a job interview for a company next week. Lets look at the AEIOU Xtra E framework and start planning what she will say in the interview. The boxes on the left are the answers to satisfy the left brain and the boxes on the right are for the right brain of the interviewer—Mr. Prasad.

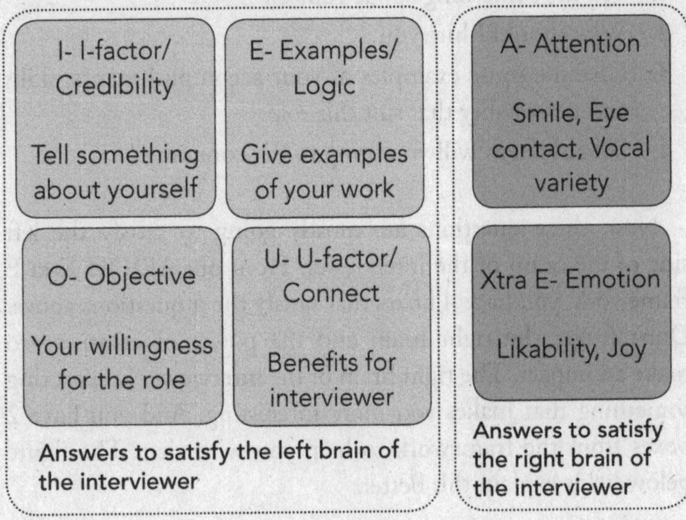

Figure 2: Pictorial representation of the framework in the interview

The Tightrope Walk

Now that you have understood what the interviewer Mr Prasad wants to hear from you as per the AEIOU Xtra E framework above, it's time to fill these boxes accordingly and make a script of your answers. Remember that a good candidate will lead the interview process and steer the interview in such a direction that it involves her strengths and capabilities. The entire process aims at fitting the candidate to the role. So your objective is to make sure that you try your level best and convey that you are the best fit for the role. The interviewer starts to gauge you the moment you enter the room. So the boxes on the right above

(Attention and Emotion) are very important. Let's now look at each of the boxes in detail.

Let's address the logical brain of Mr Prasad with the 4 out of 6 elements of the AEIOU Xtra E framework.

1. I-factor or Credibility – Typically, most interviews start with 'tell me something about yourself' or a variation of it. You are meant to demonstrate your credibility which is defined by your track record, your past work experience, your educational qualifications, skills, accomplishments, awards, and interests. This is a conversation-starter and acts as an ice-breaker for the rest of the process. But please understand that the entire interview process depends on this answer. Make sure that you summarize your resume in 4-5 lines or as briefly as possible. Don't douse your interviewer with an overload of information at this stage. You need to say just enough so that you end your answer at exactly at that point where you want the interviewer to ask the next question. As I mentioned above—lead the interview. So plan this answer in such a way that it prompts the next question that you want to be asked. (Wodtke, 2014)
2. Objective – An interview is probably the only scenario where the objective is pretty clear for both parties. But there's no harm for you, as a candidate, to explicitly say how you fit into the role and convey your willingness to work for the company. Be careful while walking the fine line between enthusiasm and over-enthusiasm. For example, the sentence 'When I read the job posting on your website, I felt that I was the perfect match for you' can be treated both ways depending on the tone. So gauge the audience and decide accordingly. Sometimes, there is no harm in trying and failing to learn. A better

way to say the same thing is 'This job posting is the right opportunity for me and I bring with myself the skills that match the requirements'. Humility is a great virtue and should be used in abundance in scenarios like these.

3. Examples/logic – Once you have broken the ice, introduced yourself, and set the objective, it is time to give a detailed answer and convince your interviewer that you are indeed the best candidate. Give stories, examples, and anecdotes from your prior experience and connect them to the job profile at hand. Please remember—the interviewer is trying to FIT you. She doesn't really care about your accomplishments unless she sees a direct fit of those accomplishments to the role she is interviewing you for. While preparing your answers, ask yourself 'How do I convince Mr Prasad that I fit the role?'. The earlier you figure this out, the easier the preparation will be. Cut the details and focus on the top 1-2 accomplishments and skills that match the profile.
4. U-factor or Connect – Mr Prasad is a human being and not a beast out to get you. Recognize that interviewers have human emotions and you can move them. Engage and connect with them. Tell them how you will benefit them and their company. They would have interviewed many people like you. Demonstrate how you stand out and make it easier for them to see the benefits of your candidature. (Martin, 2013)

Now, let's address the creative brain of Mr Prasad with the remaining 2 elements of the AEIOU Xtra E framework.

5. Attention – A warm greeting and smile, a firm handshake, a pleasant voice and a presentable, friendly personality

are the first things that can capture the interviewer's attention. Please choose an appropriate dress depending on the culture, climate, and position.

6. Emotion – This is the most underutilized area in interviews. A sincerely delivered 'thank you' to your interviewer can make them feel a lot happier and tilt the decision in your favour. Besides this, the way you answer your questions, the way you extend courtesy to them are all elements that might make the interviewer like you and feel good about you. Here is an example. If Mr Prasad is asking a question, allow him to finish first and then start your answer. It is a simple courtesy but takes you a long way. Please note that this box is also the most dangerous. If you ramble, or say something wrong that ticks the interviewer off, negative emotions kick in and you can kiss the job good bye. Make sure you trigger in them positive emotions. The simplest emotion you can give them is joy.

Here is a sample table of some of the sentences that can be used in interviews. You can also take a look at many examples on websites like Monster, etc. They have given wonderful videos on these concepts that we discuss above and have given some tips on how you can think through your answers accordingly.

Framework element	Your statement
Attention	Hello. It's really great to meet you. (with a pleasant smile and firm handshake)
Emotion	Thank you so much for inviting me for this interview and for your time. I am grateful.

Framework element	Your statement
Objective	This job is exactly what I have been looking for and I bring the following qualities that fit the profile.
Credibility	In the last 10 years at XYZ, I have done a variety of roles ranging from customer relationship to sales management. My MBA gives me a good platform to think strategically and access to the best alumni network that I can tap into for this role.
Example/ Logic	The highlight of my work at XYZ was to win a strategic account from a tough customer in Japan. It took me three months of travel to the customer site and many negotiations between our teams to make it a win-win. I got a President's award for this as well. I can speak fluent Japanese which helped me in these negotiations.
Connect	I have read about you in the business news and it's an honour to meet you. I think I can help you with the Japan and China markets to start with and help you establish a good base in these regions.

Table 1: Some examples of sentences for a job interview

When to Shut Up in an Interview

A significant focus of this book is to also help you know when NOT to say something. It's important to learn when to not shoot off your mouth, especially if you're inflicted by the foot-in-mouth syndrome. Silence really is golden sometimes. Here are some scenarios in job interviews.

1. When the interviewer is speaking or saying something – Listen to the question first. Take few seconds to make sure you heard it correctly and frame your answer, then respond. Don't start speaking while the interviewer is speaking. Shut up and listen!
2. When you are not sure or don't know the answer – You are not supposed to know everything in this world. So if you don't know the answer or are not sure just say, 'I am sorry, I don't know the answer to this'. Many times, interviewers try and corner you with questions that really are tricky. For example, I was once asked a very complicated mathematical puzzle in an interview. This puźzle had no co-relation to the role or the company or my profile. I got nervous and blabbered something. The interviewer picked on it and pushed me further till I really made a fool of myself. This is also called a stress interview; where the interviewer is trying to discern how you react under pressure.
3. When you start noticing that the interviewer is checking their watch or their phones – These little cues can say a lot. Maybe the interviewer didn't like you and is giving you a cue. So don't try too hard. Just shut up and let the interviewer close.
4. When the interview asks a question like 'what are your weaknesses' – This is a trick question. Just smile and say 'I am sorry I can't think of anything'. Or say something that is totally unrelated to the job. For example, 'food is my weakness' or 'I have trouble saying no'. Just don't give a chance to the interviewer to trap you. And for heaven's sake, avoid the following.

a. I am a perfectionist and that is my biggest weakness
b. I sometimes get angry if my peers don't do their work properly
c. I can't stand lazy people
d. I hate politics and would rather leave than deal with it
e. I work so hard that I can't manage time properly

5. When the interviewer ends the interview by asking 'do you have anything to ask me' – again, the interviewer has given you a cue that this meeting is over. Now it's best to not act cute by asking 20 questions at a time when the interviewer has pretty much ended the process. Exit gracefully and with a positive emotion, don't spoil your chances by asking the questions like the ones below and leaving a negative emotion
   a. What is my career progression in your company?
   b. What is your policy for getting a job for spouses? And how about child care and the colour of your toilet paper?
   c. What is your view on the recent FDI inflow and the risk to your company?

Communication in a conflict

In the first chapter of the book, I had given a very simple example of how conflicts can get two people adrift if we are not careful with our words. We often find ourselves in the middle of a conflict with a colleague or a customer. We cannot ignore it. You can resolve the conflict using our AEIOU Xtra E framework. The good news is that the framework can not only help you in resolving the conflict, it can also propel you further in the organization.

Let's take a very simple case so that I explain how you can use the framework to your advantage. Imagine you are Vijay, a project manager in a top company. You notice that one of your team members Ravi always comes in late to office. The office policy is 9:30 am and he never comes before 11 am. You have given him gentle reminders on the policy and discipline issue. Ravi always says that he works late till about midnight which is why he prefers to come late to office. One day, Ravi misses an important customer meeting at 10 am. You decide to talk to him. What would you say? I did this role play in my class and asked students to play Vijay and Ravi.

Role play number 1

Vijay: Good morning Ravi. I want to talk to you. Can you come in to my office?

Ravi enters

Vijay: You missed an important meeting today at 10 am. Despite giving you repeated warnings, you continue to come late. You need to do something about this or else I will have to take action.

Ravi: I have told you that I work till midnight for the customer. The entire module is on my shoulders. I had asked you to hire an extra engineer but you said that the costs don't justify. I cannot deliver the module and also come to office on time. You can find somebody else.

What happened here? How did a simple conversation result in a conflict and end in a deadlock? I asked the student who played the role of Ravi. He said that he didn't like the tone Vijay used. He sounded very rude and arrogant. And he also threatened to take action.

Role play number 2

Vijay sends an mail to Ravi—Hi Ravi, whenever you get the time, please see me. I need to talk to you regarding the attendance policy which I have discussed with you earlier as well.

Ravi enters

Vijay: Is everything okay Ravi? Didn't see you in the 10 am call today.

Ravi: I am fine. I was working late last night and am sorry I missed the call. There is too much work and I had requested you to hire an additional engineer.

Ajay: I will try, Ravi. But it looks tough. The deadlines are approaching and your module is quite critical. Budgets are flat and I don't have the resources to hire.

Ravi: Then you suggest something. I don't think I can meet the deadlines and also come to office on time.

Vijay: I think you need to take time management training. When I was your age, I could handle twice the work you are doing and I would always come to office on time.

I stopped the role play and asked both students to talk about how they feel. In this case, the student who played Ravi said that he felt as if Ajay was trying to be his Dad. And he didn't like how Vijay belittled his work.

There were at least 3 more scenarios that stood out for this case. In one scenario, Ravi just stormed out of the room in anger. In another, Vijay showed his anger by using words like 'I am the manager and if I say that you come at 9:30, you come at 9:30!' And in one bizarre case, Ravi threatened back 'I will complain to the HR manager that you are harassing me'. Now it's possible that my students got a bit carried away. But I think the reality is not very different. Conflicts are caused by poor choice of words and wrong tone of voice. Many times they are unintentional. And many times, they result in serious damage to relationships and corporate culture. Let's take a look at how the framework of AEIOU Xtra E used by Vijay actually worked on Ravi's mind.

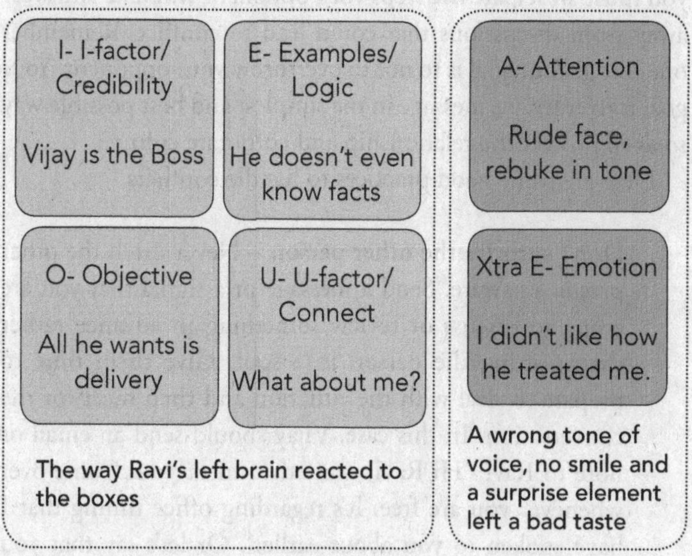

Figure 3: Effect of the framework on the receiver

As you can see in the figure above, despite the good intentions of Vijay, the way Ravi's mind reacted to the words of Ravi led to a conflict.

Now, let us not forget that Vijay has a job to do. And in this case, Ravi did do something that was against the corporate discipline. Why did he not accept his mistake and apologize? Maybe, Vijay was miffed when Ravi started to counter argue and the emotional burst could have caused Vijay to say things he shouldn't have. In the scenario that we discussed above of

Vijay confronting Ravi for coming late to office, both Vijay and Ravi must know how to deal with this type of situation.

So how does one deal with conflicts? And how does one choose words carefully so that conflicts get resolved as amicably as possible. It is like a game of chess. As a player of this game, you must anticipate the steps your opponent will take and steer away from discussions that could lead to conflict. Remember one thing. Your goal is to not to overthrow your opponent. Your goal is to convey a message in the simplest and best possible way so as to protect the relationship and corporate culture.

Here are some good practices to handle conflicts.

1. **Don't surprise the other person** – Never catch the other person unaware. Send a message or a signal that you are going to discuss or review something in advance rather than putting the person in a spot. Give them time to prepare to deal with the situation and then meet for the conversation. In this case, Vijay should send an email or note to Ravi, 'Hi Ravi, wanted to meet you. Come over whenever you are free. It's regarding office timing that I have spoken to you about earlier'. Or let's say that you don't have the luxury of sending a signal like this and the situation demands that you tackle the issue right then and there. In that case say something like 'This might be a surprise and I'm sorry to put you in a spot. But I thought it best to get this out of our way'.
2. **Focus on the issue and not the personality** – Stick to the issue. In this case, the issue is office timing. Avoid mixing the customer deadlines and new IT policy and the latest budget laws to the topic. Ravi's personality has nothing to do with it. Keep away from it. Avoid too much clutter and keep the issue simple.

3. **Keep room for negotiation** – Often, there is scope for resolution if you are willing to negotiate. A loss to the other party is a defeat of the entire objective. It is also a defeat of an entire corporate culture. Maybe Ravi and Vijay could have come to a middle ground in that meeting. And if that means win-win for both, why not. Both parties must be willing to bend a little to gain a lot. For example, Ravi could be allowed late walk-ins for some days but he must ensure his presence for all pre-scheduled meetings.
4. **Get your facts right** – Logic and data are very important for these kind of conversations. Vijay must dig the attendance records to see the exact situation himself. Maybe the fact that Ravi stays at work till midnight can be probed further to see what exactly he does so late? This might give Vijay scope to confront Ravi and reach a resolution. Truth and facts are strong ammunition for your case. So go prepared.
5. **Know when to shut up and break the process if it is unproductive** – You must know when to shut up, listen to the other person, and when to break the meeting. When tempers rise, the harm can be controlled if one of them says, 'I think this meeting is starting to get unproductive. Why don't we take a break and meet again?' A break can calm tempers down and put things into perspective. So use them till you reach a resolution.
6. **Maintain a calm face and friendly tone** – This is by far the most important part of the framework. Try and be calm and avoid raising your tone.

Framework for Vijay

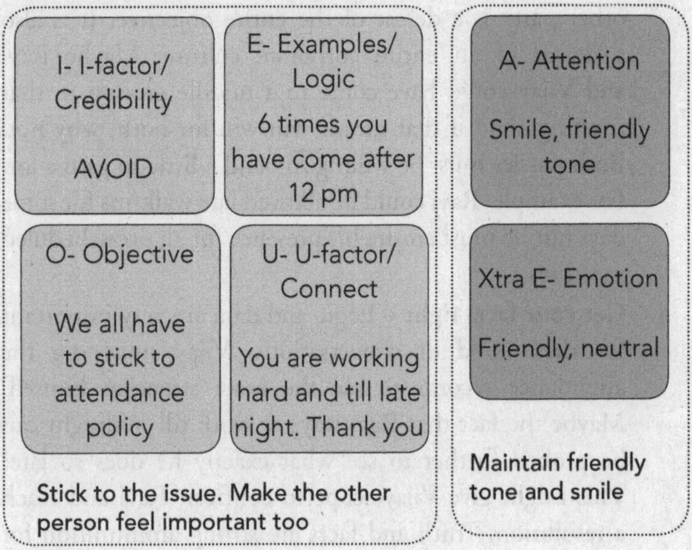

Figure 4: Vijay's framework for conflict

So here is how Vijay can start the conversation using this framework

Hi Ravi, I know you are working quite hard for this customer. Thank you for this. But we have a clear attendance policy and I request you to adhere to it.

Now if Ravi is sensible and applies the framework properly and knows that he has no choice but to follow company policy, he should accept and act accordingly. If I were Ravi, I would even apologize and use the following framework.

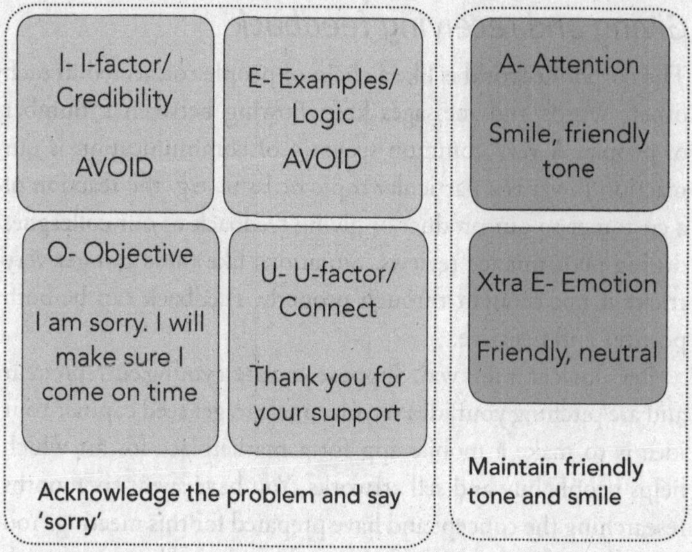

Figure 5: Ravi's framework for the conflict

Hopefully both Vijay and Ravi will leave the room with a resolution. There could be two complications however:

1. Ravi takes it very badly and throws the conversation into a spin—In this case, break the conversation and revisit this at a later time.
2. The situation hits a deadlock—In this case, stick to your ground and do what is expected out of a manager of your organization. There is a code of conduct and you must enforce it with the help of the HR department.

Giving and receiving feedback

The corporate world is like a chain of people connected to each other. Words and messages keep flowing between a number of people. A very common scenario of communication is our reaction towards a particular topic or issue, e.g. the reaction of a customer to our product or giving feedback to our colleagues during performance reviews. Situations like these can get very tricky if not thought through properly. Feedback can be both positive and negative.

Let's look at it this way. Suppose you are a young entrepreneur and are pitching your idea to your uncle to get seed capital. Your idea is to make a mobile app for a marketplace for art which helps people buy and sell artworks. You have spent six months researching the concept and have prepared for this meeting. You expect your uncle to ask you questions on business potential, risks, etc. Instead, he right away starts criticizing your idea. He first rubbishes the concept, then points out three things where he knows the idea will fall apart, and finally says no. You are crushed and shattered. Your uncle has not rejected your idea, but has also killed your spirit. Your uncle is just one of the many examples we see every day where finding faults is considered a virtue and many dreams are trampled on unwittingly.

It would have been helpful if the uncle could have given some feedback on the merits of the idea, the areas where he thinks you need to refocus and encouraged you to come back in a month's time with revised data; you would have been stimulated to take the idea forward. Even if he didn't give the money, you might be encouraged to try asking someone else.

It is important to be careful while doling out feedback to others. I will talk about how to receive feedback later. Some points to keep in mind while giving feedback are as follows.

1. Give feedback only when you have been asked – Nobody likes to receive unsolicited feedback. In our culture, we feel free to present opinions on every topic—even if we are not experts in that area. Clearly a lot of us believe that we can be better prime ministers if given a chance and can play better cricket than the current crop of cricketers if we are put in the stadium. Give feedback ONLY when explicitly solicited.
2. Don't nitpick – Make sure that you first examine the subject from all angles and form a balanced opinion. Avoid finding faults all the time. Find something good first and then look for areas of improvement. One of the best examples of this is how Masterchef eliminates a cook. The judges praise this person on how well she or he did in the competition so far. They highlight their strengths and also make them feel good about being in the show. They finally give them a fitting farewell from the program which is emotionally uplifting instead of breaking them down.
3. Treat others with respect – Nobody likes to hear negative things about oneself or about our products that we had created with so much passion. So when you are giving a negative feedback to others, remember how you would like to be treated first. Treat others with dignity and don't leave them bruised and broken with your harsh words.
4. Use 'I think' sentences – You are conveying your opinion and not passing a judgement. Many times I have heard people say sentences which begin like, 'We think…' No, you don't. There are journalists on national television who make sweeping statements and ask big questions like 'India wants to know…' And we all know that India doesn't really care about that at all. So use sentences with 'I think', 'In my opinion', or 'I feel'.

While receiving feedback, it is imperative to listen. Don't justify and don't interrupt the person who is giving the feedback. Thank them for doing a just analysis and spending time to give you feedback. After all, their intention is to help you (or your product/concept) become better. Good companies go to lengths to collect feedback from their customers. And many feel that only those who care for you will take the time to give feedback. So they would read all of them carefully and sometimes even write back to customers saying that their feedback was valuable and has been incorporated.

Handling tricky situations

If you have never bungled things up in your business or corporate life, then something is very wrong. It is unnatural. Landing oneself in difficult situations is a given in the corporate scenario. And as a manager and future leader, you will have to deal with these situations and convey an appropriate message to the affected parties. These affected parties could be your customers or your internal employees as well. The entire world would keenly watch and follow what you do. One of the best examples of how a leader can help a country with his reassuring message is Barack Obama. His words on the night of the Connecticut shootings in a school, where many children died, were very emotional and hit the mark. They sounded genuine and Obama shed a tear that day. (Obama, 2012)

> We've endured too many of these tragedies in the past few years. And each time I learn the news, I react not as a President, but as anybody else would—as a parent. And that was especially true today. I know there's not a parent in America who doesn't feel the same overwhelming grief that I do.

The majority of those who died today were children—beautiful little kids between the ages of 5 and 10 years old. They had their entire lives ahead of them—birthdays, graduations, weddings, kids of their own. Among the fallen were also teachers—men and women who devoted their lives to helping our children fulfill their dreams.

So our hearts are broken today—for the parents and grandparents, sisters and brothers of these little children, and for the families of the adults who were lost. Our hearts are broken for the parents of the survivors as well, for as blessed as they are to have their children home tonight, they know that their children's innocence has been torn away from them too early, and there are no words that will ease their pain.

As a country, we have been through this too many times. Whether it's an elementary school in Newtown, or a shopping mall in Oregon, or a temple in Wisconsin, or a movie theater in Aurora, or a street corner in Chicago—these neighborhoods are our neighborhoods, and these children are our children. And we're going to have to come together and take meaningful action to prevent more tragedies like this, regardless of the politics.

This evening, Michelle and I will do what I know every parent in America will do, which is hug our children a little tighter and we'll tell them that we love them, and we'll remind each other how deeply we love one another. But there are families in Connecticut who cannot do that tonight. And they need all of us right now. In the hard days to come, that community needs us to be at our best as Americans. And I will do everything in my power as President to help.

In the words above, Obama connected with every family in the US, gave examples and logic and demonstrated his credibility as the President of USA. His voice and face conveyed a very balanced appeal to convey the seriousness and the emotions were visible. How many of us could say these words? How many leaders will even stand up and make a statement where one exposes his personal side so honestly? It was a very difficult situation to be in, but he handled it very well. He did not take the focus of the issue away from the heinous crime, kept the sensitivity of lives lost, and hinted on the horrors of not having a stronger restriction on the sales of guns in USA.

In a wonderful article called 'Sabha Chaturya' or 'Tact in King's Court', Devdutt Pattanaik explains how wise men would use tact and wit to handle difficult situations with the King. Imagine you work as a finance minister in the King's court. The King has appointed the Queen's brother in your office without discussing with you. He is very incompetent. This is a very tricky situation and requires tact to handle it properly. If you don't use tact, you might step on the wrong side of the King and lose everything. (Pattanaik, 2010). In many ways, we land up in similar situations with our customers, bosses and people who are very important to us and our business. So how does one deal with such situations and handle it with words. Let us consider the following scenarios

1. Conveying a bad news
2. Saying no

Conveying a bad news

It is not easy to convey bad news to someone because there is no easy way to do it. There is usually no way to sugarcoat it or make it better. Imagine if you are a manager in a big organization which is not doing so well. It has been decided that few members of your team have to be let go from their service to control the costs. Now you have to go and break this news to the members of your team. Those members might react very badly to this news. They might even break down or throw an emotional fit. Given such a scenario, how does the manager say these words? Well, if you think this job is hard, think about the people who work in healthcare. Imagine being a doctor and delivering bad news to a family. The AEIOU Xtra E framework can help you to convey the most appropriate message in this situation. Here is how you can prepare.

1. Objective – Your objective is not only to convey the message but to also minimize the anxiety of the audience.
2. U-factor/Connect – The audience is greatly affected here. So you need to ensure that you put yourself in the shoes of the audience and be very careful of how you word the message. Words like 'I am really sorry that you have to go through this' are apt to show that you are empathetic towards their feelings.
3. Examples/Logic – find ways to address the anxiety of the audience. For example, if you are conveying a news to the person that he has lost his job, then address what you have in store for him on managing his transition. Many good companies offer a package. This is a time to explain that. Just the message 'You don't have a job' will crush the person. So a message 'You don't have a job and here are 3 things we have for you to manage this difficult phase' is a better message.
4. I-factor/Credibility – Avoid this box completely.
5. Attention – Declare that you are going to announce bad news. Make sure your face and gestures are calm and demonstrate the seriousness of the message.

6. Emotions – Avoid any word or sentence that can flare up the emotions of the audience. Keep it on a neutral phase. Words like 'I am sorry to bring you this news' or 'I am sorry that things didn't work out' are good ways to convey empathy and minimize anxiety.

Some best practices while giving bad news are

1. Make your audience sit down before you give the message. The news might shock them and they may be unsteady on their feet. When they are seated, the body and mind are able to cope with the news better.
2. Avoid surprises. Announce in advance that you are going to bring an unfortunate message. The more you prepare your audience to digest the news, the better it is.

Saying No

This one is a very difficult one. I must admit that till today, I cannot say no to some people. In many companies, the culture does not support an employee to say no to a superior or a senior. Even in many cultures like Japan, saying no to a customer is very hard—almost impossible. Having said that, it does not mean that we should say yes to everything. It is not good for us and for the other person. This scenario is almost similar to the one above—where we have to give bad news. No is a bad news to the other person. Here are some suggestions on how you can say no.

1. Convey 'no' without using the word 'no' – My first book *Plunnge* was rejected by many publications. Many of them didn't even bother to respond. So silence was considered rejection. But one wrote a wonderful message back. 'Dear Mr Godhwani, I thoroughly enjoyed reading the

manuscript. But unfortunately, our portfolio of books is very different and we don't feel *Plunnge* will fit the same. I wish you all the best....' If you notice, there is not a single mention of 'no'. But the 'no' is conveyed very cleverly with the 'but unfortunately' and 'we don't feel *Plunnge* will fit the same' sentences. A similar strategy is used by many Venture Capitalists who say no to budding entrepreneurs. The 'no' is conveyed in a way that does not dishearten the entrepreneur and they feel encouraged to try elsewhere.

2. Avoid lengthy explanations for 'no' – Your role is to convey a polite 'no'. Avoid giving lengthy explanations on why you are saying 'no'. I find many students who reject a company's job offer mentioning things like 'I am not taking this offer because the salary is very low and I have taken a loan. So if I calculate my monthly salary and take out cost of living in Bangalore, I won't be able to pay my EMI.' I find such messages very funny, amateurish, and preposterous. Never ever provide more information than what the audience has time for.

Saying sorry

In September 2014, Flipkart announced a 'Big Billion Day Sale' scheduled for 6 October and aggressively campaigned throughout the country. The founders Sachin and Binny Bansal personally wrote to their customers about this mega sale in an email.

> *To celebrate Flipkart's journey, we are going to have a sale to end all sales. The Big Billion Day Sale is on the 6-10-2014....and the date is no coincidence.*
>
> *The day 6-10 marks the number of the flat we started out from. And holding India's biggest ever sale on that day is our*

tribute to dreams and dreamers. It's also our way of making sure all our customers dreams come true.

On this day, you will have over 70 categories to shop from, with flash sales, deals of the hour, lucky draws every hour and unprecedented offers and discounts to look forward to.

The entire country eagerly awaited this day. I know my friends and students had already planned what to buy and were excited. Flipkart had planned for months and had kept about 10000 people on call to make deliveries. India was awakening to a new dawn brought by 2 young engineers who had the guts to fight giants like Amazon and many other e-tailers. Sadly, the day was a disaster. The servers crashed and customers were disappointed. They vented out their anger on social media and termed the day 'Big Billion Disaster. Flipkart was called 'Flopkart'. The next day, Sachin and Binny sent a public apology to everyone. I received one too. Here is what it said.

Yesterday was a big day for us. And we really wanted it to be a great day for you. But at the end of the day, we know that your experience was less than pleasant. We did not live up to the promises we made and for that we are really and truly sorry.

An unprecedented 1.5 million people shopped at Flipkart yesterday. While we stand humbled by the sheer faith that such a large number of customers have shown in us, we are unhappy that we were unable to live up to the expectations of millions more who wanted to buy from us yesterday.

And this is not acceptable to us.

It takes an enormous amount of strength and courage to stand up and apologize for your mistakes in front of the whole world. 'I am sorry' are very powerful and persuasive words that have to be said at the right time. The impact of these words on the audiences is magical. It lowers the anger and helps take the situation towards a positive side. I read a wonderful analysis of this apology on social media that called this the gold standard of apology. (Soundarajan, 2014) Soundarajan, R., 2014. Flipkart Apology: A gold standard indeed. [Online] Available at: http://www.afaqs.com/all/news/case_studies/reports/331/FLASH/index.htm

Here's how we can use the AEIOU Xtra E framework to apologize to an audience.

1. Objective – Use the words 'I apologize' or 'I am sorry' explicitly.
2. U-factor/Connect – Tell the audience how much they suffered because of your mistake.
3. Examples/Logic – Explain why the mistake happened. Give them a logic that is clear. In Flipkart's case, the Bansals explained the server failure and it made sense. The audience knows that there are times when things don't work. A good explanation of why they didn't work is of immense help here. Many high-tech companies use this very well. The famous Intel Integer flaw is a case in point you could look at.
4. I-factor/Credibility – Stand by your credibility and make your words demonstrate that you value the trust your audience has in you.
5. Attention – No need for this here. The audience is already very angry and there is high attention on your issue.
6. Emotions – Have a very calm and neutral face. The tone should be somber and mellow. When you say the words 'Sorry', your tone must be apologetic and genuine.

Chapter 13

Communication for Entrepreneurs

One might argue that the world of entrepreneurs is similar to that of a people working in the corporate sector. And hence their communication needs should be similar. That is not true though. An entrepreneur faces more challenges than the person who works in the corporate sector and hence we take up this chapter to address the unique needs of an entrepreneur. First, they have to do everything themselves. Second, they really don't have the safety net of the big corporate company and third, they are hungrier to get things done. In this chapter, we will look at how to apply the AEIOU Xtra E framework of persuasive communication for various scenarios of an entrepreneur's world.

I got hooked to the world of entrepreneurship when I was working in a big tech MNC and my job involved finding and engaging companies who would make applications for mobile phones. I was amazed by entrepreneurs and they were so much fun to work with. Majority of them would operate out of their homes, survive on shoestring budgets, and displayed unmatched dedication to their work. In many ways they were like ascetics standing on one foot, striving to reach their goal through tough penance. The world would laugh at them, but they wouldn't lose focus. For entrepreneurs, communication and persuasion are much needed skills. They can use it for any of the following.

- Pitching to investors to raise money
- Selling product/services to a customer—usually a cold call

In this chapter, we will deal with these two important scenarios with the AEIOU and Xtra E framework.

Pitching to an investor

One of the most common challenges for entrepreneurs is to raise money from investors, high net individuals, angels, friends, or sometimes even family members. Getting funding is not easy. Hence, this scenario requires a lot of preparation and effort on the entrepreneur's part before he is ready to make the pitch. This word 'pitch' comes from Baseball where the pitcher pitches to the batsman. (Elsbach, 2003). It is also used in a phrase called 'elevator pitch' for situations where time is very limited. There is a bit of an urban legend of how the phrase elevator pitch evolved which involves a smart entrepreneur, a big businessman, and paucity of time. Once, a young, smart entrepreneur was trying to get an appointment with a rich, important person to get him to invest in his idea. He tried several times but the secretary told him that his calendar was full for next three months. He kept trying though and finally the secretary gave in and said that he has time to pitch his idea in the elevator which the businessman took from the ground floor to his penthouse office. The elevator took less than a minute to reach the office. That's probably where the phrase 'elevator pitch' comes from. It has come to mean a succinct, pithy description which conveys the business idea.

There is another similar legend I have heard. A young businessman wanted to meet the Prime Minister of a country. He wanted to discuss some policies that could help the country and entrepreneurs like him. He kept calling the office of the

PM and the secretary kept pushing the request. The secretary finally gave him time to come and meet the PM when he walked out of his home to the car in the morning—which was less than 30 seconds. The businessman said, 'That is plenty'. The next day, the businessman waited outside the PM's home patiently. The businessman greeted him and said, 'Mr PM, I have 100 million USD from the recent profits I made from the petrochemical industry. I need your advice on how to invest it in your country.' The PM looked at his secretary, who was standing right next to the businessman, and said, 'Bring this man to my office at 10 am tomorrow.'

A pitch is used very commonly in business context. A pitch is typically short and persuasive. It is made on occasions when either the audience is busy and where it isn't possible to indulge in details. So the message has to hit home run in a matter of seconds. If it doesn't, chances are that your objective will remain unfulfilled, which means that if you're an entrepreneur, you won't get the money from this investor.

THE PREPARATION

In this scenario of pitching to an investor, the entrepreneur has to make some extra preparations before the AEIOU Xtra E framework can kick in.

Deeper understanding of the audience

We had discussed the importance of audience research in Chapter 3. This research helps in preparing for the message that is suitable for the audience. In this case, entrepreneurs need to go deeper and find out the following about the investors.

- **How do they decide what company to invest in** – Most investors are now very open about what they are looking for when it comes to investing in a business. They have a professional company with a website which can give you a lot of information about them—what they are looking for in an entrepreneur, what other companies they have invested in, etc. Many of these investors are very focused on a particular sector. So if your business idea relates to the healthcare industry and the investor is more focused on the education space, you may want to recoup and approach someone more relevant to your sector.

- **What excites them** – Every person is passionate about something. And for investors, it shouldn't be a top secret. Google search might give you lot of information on the topics that excite them. You can look at their blogs, read interviews about them to get a better insight into their thought process.
- **What questions they have** – Just like how we discussed in earlier chapters, the investors too have the following questions in their minds.

  - Who are you and what is your idea
  - What kind of investment are you looking for
  - Why is this idea different/Prove your point (Convince me)
  - What's the exit plan or ROI for my investments

A good demo of your product

A good investor will not invest until they see an actual proof of your concept. Gone are the days where investors would listen to someone in a coffee shop, look at their plan on the paper napkin, and tear off a check. So make sure you prepare a good prototype or a demo that showcases your product to the investors. A well-thought demo is very important for your pitch. You may not have time to show it entirely, probably due to paucity of time, but fortune favours the prepared.

Find a connection to introduce you to the investor

An investor gets hundreds of proposals every day. Emails inundate him, he hears proposals at conferences, parties, business meets—these are all entrepreneurs who pitch him a lot of ideas. So your chances of winning his attention are higher if you reach him through somebody he knows closely. This step is not mandatory. But since your credibility is very low, a common friend might fatten up that box of the framework. So prepare well and find a common connection who can make the introduction. This is plain business. The investor will invest only when they see money in you. But there is no harm in making that extra effort to go through a trusted source to increase your credibility.

Prepare for rejection

The failure of your pitch does not always mean that your pitch was bad. It could be because this investor is not really the right audience for you. Or it could be that the timing of the idea is not right. Or maybe the investor is really not in a good mood to invest today. In a conference I attended in the Bay Area in May 2014, an investor spoke about how he rejected a pitch from an entrepreneur called Larry Page. And how he will repent this decision all his life. Larry Page then went on to found Google with Sergei Brin and made billions for his investors. So the equation between the entrepreneur and investors is like chemistry. It can click, but can also flop badly. So don't really take the rejections to your heart. Have a positive attitude and try elsewhere. Imagine that you are a fisherman. If you didn't find the fish at one spot of the lake, just move to another spot and try again. There are enough spots in the lake to fish.

THE FRAMEWORK

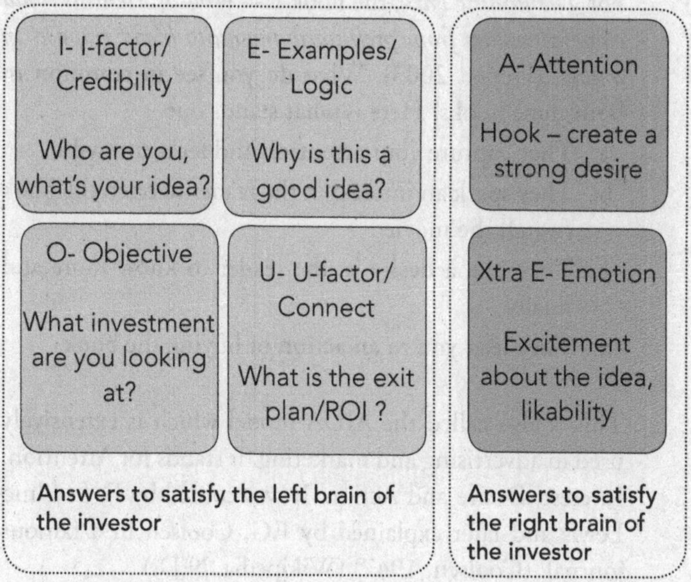

Once your framework looks solid, start working on what the investor wants to know and what each of the boxes should include.

1. **Attention: the hook** – A big difference in this scenario from a job interview is the Attention box. In a pitch to an investor, you really have to hook them to listen to you further. The hook is required to draw the investor into your idea. Imagine yourself walking into a book store. Don't you pick a book by looking at its cover and then turn it over to read the short description on what it is

about? Let me give you a few examples of 2 of my faviorite books—*The Bourne Identity* and *The Jurassic Park*. Here is the hook of *The Bourne Identity—What if a man with amnesia has forgotten he's the world's most dangerous assassin?* For *The Jurassic Park*, the hook is—*What if scientists could clone dinosaurs from prehistoric mosquito blood trapped in amber.* (Finder, 2003). What do you see in common in both these hooks? Here is what stands out

a. They capture your **attention** and let it run wild
b. They spark an **interest** in the reader to open the book /watch the movie
c. They fuel a **desire** in the reader to know more and finally
d. They lead you to an **action** of buying the book

This is also called the AIDA model which is extensively used in advertising and marketing. It stands for Attention, Interest, Desire and Action. It was coined by E. St Elmo Lewis and later explained by F.G. Coolsen in a famous journal. (Coolsen, 1947) (Wikipedia, N.D.)

2. **Objective** – While it is very clear that you are meeting the investor for his money, it still helps to state the objective clearly by remembering the SMART guidelines we discussed earlier. Combine the objective with the connect box to help the investor see the benefits in investing in your business.
3. **U-factor/Connect** – It is the investor's job to invest in a scheme that provides better returns. So this is the place where you as an entrepreneur who is pitching to the investor, can connect your objective and lay out the benefit the investor will get from your proposal. Some

investors may want to first understand the idea better. So go to the homework stage and see what kind of investor you are dealing with. This is not an algorithm where every step has to be followed step-by-step. Be willing to innovate and improvise.

4. **Examples/logic**—This is where the demo of your idea and product is extremely important. The preparation you have done beforehand will help you immensely here; and remember to employ the story telling style we discussed earlier. Avoid too much jargon or tech speak and try to make the concept simple for the investor. They are typically interested to know the following.
   a. Why has this idea never been done before
   b. What is so unique about it
   c. Have you tried the product on an actual scenario

5. **I-factor/Credibility** – If you have done your preparation well and a mutual friend has put you in touch with an investor, then you need not fret too much about credibility. Avoid over-emphasis of your past or educational backgrounds in this phase. This is not a job interview. By design, an entrepreneur does not have credibility. And investors would be aware if it is your first startup; but if you have a track record in starting up and are a serial entrepreneur, then definitely talk about it. If I were an investor, I would love to hear an entrepreneur who is not cagey about his failures. Don't hide your failures. Talk about them and mention what you learnt from them.

   Emotions – If you have hooked the investor, and have taken them to the Desire phase of the AIDA model that I mentioned above, then that means that you are on the right track for this box. You can convey happiness or excitement to your investment through your demo. Avoid irritating them by using sensational words, MBA jargon, and complicated spread sheets.

Framework element	Your statement
Attention/Hook	What if we could use drones to deliver pizzas in Bangalore. Imagine that all your friends decide to plonk at your place for the IPL match. Everybody is hungry and Pizza Hut says that they will take minimum 45 minutes to deliver.
Emotion	I am really excited to be a part of this commerce revolution and invite you to join.
Objective	I am looking for a series 2 funding of $100 million in return for a 10 percent stake in my company. This money will be used to setup a manufacturing plant in Mysore and establish the supply chain to ship the drones worldwide.
Credibility	I built my first solar powered flying car at the age of 10 and got the Intel Science award.
Example/Logic	Every day, 18000 pizzas are delivered in Bangalore by about 800 delivery boys. About 22 percent orders are turned down because of lack of delivery boys in peak hours of lunch and dinner. By using

Framework element	Your statement
	Drones, Pizza Hut can increase sales and create a revolution by delivering pizzas in 12 minutes.
Connect	I already have orders from 3 top clients. I have a letter of intent from Amazon India as well and am doing a pilot with HAL for a defense contract.

Table 1: Some examples of sentences for a pitch

When to Shut up in a Pitch

There are times where we need to restrain ourselves from opening our mouths. Here are some scenarios in a pitch (many of them are quite similar to the job interviews part).

1. When the investor is speaking or saying something—Listen to the question first. Take few seconds to make sure you heard it right and frame your answer and respond. Don't start speaking while the investor is speaking. Shut up and listen!
2. When you are not sure or don't know the answer—You are not supposed to know everything in this world. So if you don't know the answer or are not sure just say 'I am sorry. I don't know the answer'. Many times, investors try and corner you with questions that really are tricky. For example, an investor might ask you 'What is the market opportunity of your idea?' You are an entrepreneur and you may not have thought through that beyond a point. Sometimes, if you truly believe in the product and have

piloted it with some very exciting results, that should tell you about the potential of your product. Which entrepreneur would know the potential of a drone today? This is a very futuristic vision and you may not even know it's potential. Be honest.

3. When you start noticing that the investor is checking their watch or their phones – These little cues can say a lot. Maybe the investor didn't like you and is giving you a cue. So don't try too hard. Just shut up and let the investor close.
4. When they bluntly say no – Just shut up, thank them for their time, and walk away. Avoid explaining to them that they are making a huge mistake by not investing in you. They are experts and if they don't see value in your idea, your argument might make it worse and generate a negative emotion.

Cold calling a potential customer

One of the joys of entrepreneurship is to be able to pick the phone and call potential customers who will buy your product. This is an excellent way to garner early feedback. Thanks to the tele-marketing people though, this is getting increasingly difficult because the other person might not even pick an unknown number. Many times you don't have a mutual friend to connect you. And emails are ignored. So how does one reach this important customer. Let us assume that you are the entrepreneur who makes drones and you want to pitch your idea to the CEO of Pizza Hut India. Through some means, you have been able to get his cell phone number. Now what do you do? How do you handle this situation? Well, fret not! All sales people go through this and it is termed a 'cold call'. Cold calling is the sales process of approaching prospective customers or clients—typically via telephone, by email, or by making a connection on a social network—who were not expecting such an interaction. The word 'cold' is used because the person receiving the call is not expecting a call or has not specifically asked to be contacted by a sales person. A cold call is usually the start of a sales process and can result in a meeting with the client to take the discussion further. The telemarketing industry uses it every day for selling insurances, credit cards, and a host of unwanted products. If they can do it, I am sure we all can learn too, and better. In this section, I will highlight how to go about the cold calling scenario using our AEIOU and Xtra E framework.

1. **Attention: the hook** – A cold call is quite similar to a pitch with the only difference that you are doing the conversation over a phone or an email. So it requires a lot more tact for the hook to generate the AIDA effect. A great idea which I learnt from a friend of mine is the SMS. My friend does not directly make a call. He first sends a text which is a hook in itself. An example of this text is 'Dear Mr Sharma, I got your number from Dinesh who is a common friend, he might have mentioned me. I request 5 minutes of your time to talk about my venture when convenient. Rgds Ashok'. It is concise and hits the mark. And he usually gets a response with a time to call him. And on the phone, he continues the hook further and uses the pitch principals we discussed above.
2. **Objective** – The main objective of a cold call is to either get more time from the customer or from the right person in his team. But make sure that you send her all the brochures, product videos, and collaterals before you make that call, so they have some information about it.

3. **Examples/logic** – The collaterals and videos are very critical here. A picture or a visual communicates better than plain words. So invest lot of time to make good visuals and send them.

All the remaining elements of the AEIOU Xtra E framework besides the 3 mentioned above—the U-factor or Connect, the I-factor or Credibility, and the Emotions are exactly the same as we discussed in making a pitch. So I will not mention them again here.

Chapter 14

Communication in the Social Setting

Imagine a typical day at office. You enter the office building and run into your CEO who is also waiting for the lift. You have few minutes to make an impression—build stronger ties with him. Once you reach your desk, you meet many more colleagues in the aisles and exchange pleasantries. During coffee and lunch breaks you have opportunities to network with your colleagues from other departments who are important to your work. And in the evening, you are invited to an office party. Later in the month, you are to travel to a customer site and also attend a conference. Each of these scenarios is a golden opportunity to build your presence and demonstrate your leadership qualities to your colleagues, customers, and the world. And that is what we will discuss in this chapter—the importance of AEIOU Xtra E framework in socializing with our colleagues and customers. Some of the scenarios are.

1. Making a first impression
2. Interacting in an informal setup—in the aisles, cafeteria
3. The art of networking with internal and external stakeholders
4. A corporate party or a social get together with colleagues or an offsite activity

5. Presence in meetings, conferences
6. Communicating with media

THE IMPORTANCE OF SOCIALIZING

We spend most of our waking time in office, communicating with our colleagues. We also attend conferences, parties, farewell lunches, and offsites with them. These are all excellent opportunities to build ammo for two of the boxes of your framework. The first is the **I box of credibility** and the second is **U box of connect**. Let me explain how. We take our example of Ajay who is supposed to make a presentation to the CEO and his staff. We had done the following analysis of the AEIOU Xtra E framework for him as shown in the figure below.

Now if you can see from the framework, you will realize that the 'I' and 'U' boxes are dangerously weak. So Ajay needs to utilize the next two weeks to find a way to meet the CEO or his staff members in an informal settings like the cafeteria, or the lobby, and build his credibility and connect with them. I think then he will have a much better chance of winning the presentation. Please realize that till that moment of his presentation in that room, the CEO or his staff doesn't even know that he exists. So Ajay should a way to interact with the CEO in the 2 weeks he has—this could be just by bumping into him at the coffee machine or water dispenser or in the hallway or the lobby.

A presentation in front of a CEO in a board room and a meeting with the CEO near the cafeteria are 2 separate instances of demonstrating your presence and applying the same framework to your advantage. Both scenarios are not exactly a pitch or a presentation. To me, these are essential social skills that must be discussed as an academic framework and cannot

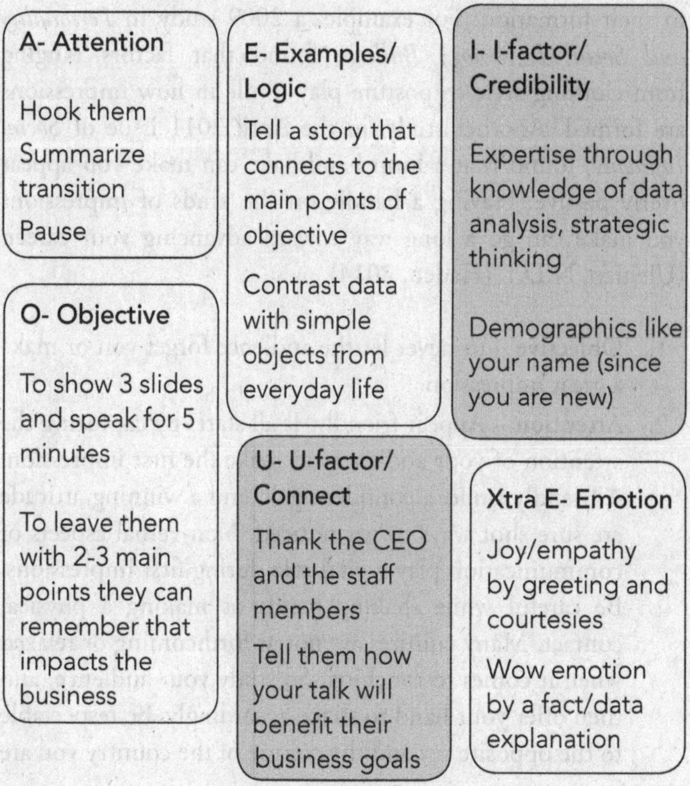

Figure 1: The complete AEIOU Xtra E framework for Ajay

be disassociated as a separate subject. That is the whole purpose of this book as well—to have 1 framework apply to multiple contexts.

1. Making a first impression

It's true, unfair as it may be, first impressions can be lasting. Substantial research has affirmed the importance of first impressions while exploring a variety of factors that contribute to their formation. For example, a 2009 study in *Personality and Social Psychology Bulletin* found that factors ranging from clothing style to posture play a role in how impressions are formed. Another study, in the April 2011 issue of *Social Influence,* found that a limp handshake can make you appear overly passive. Having a handle on the kinds of impressions you make can go a long way toward advancing your career. (Uleman, N.D.). (Haden, 2014)

1. **Objective** – to never let the audience forget you or make a great impression
2. **Attention** – Appear friendly. It all starts by capturing the attention of your audiences to make the first impression. A friendly smile, a confident gait, and a winning attitude are sure shot ways to get noticed. Non-verbal aspects of communication play a vital role during first impressions. Be careful while shaking hands or making a physical contact. Many cultures are not as forthcoming or relaxed when it comes to touching. So study your audience, and then offer your hand to shake accordingly. Be respectable to the opposite sex and the culture of the country you are in.
3. **Credibility** – avoid over-selling. Avoid over-selling yourself or your views to your audience, especially when you are making a first impression. Nothing can be a worse put-off than a person who is in your face in the first meeting. I will give you few examples from my own experiences on how over-selling can be disastrous. I was in a dinner with some colleagues who were from different countries and cultures all over the world. It was a light evening and we were all meeting for the first time. There was this one person who was very loud and kept talking

about how he is winning customers in his geography. He started throwing names and was full of himself. The next day, he was the butt of all our jokes and clearly made a very poor impression on all of us. Another example is that of someone I knew and who is always looking at making a quick buck. He has a day job, but dabbles in real estate and direct selling of Amway products in his spare time. And boy! We all dread having to talk to him. In the first meeting I had with him in the park near our locality, he cornered me and kept on selling his Amway products. Now I avoid going to the park if I spot him there. He could be a wonderful person, but it is difficult to get past his salesman persona. When you have to make your first impressions, your visiting card is enough to build your credibility. If you are friendly-looking, as what we discussed in the point above, you really don't have to work hard on this point. Sometimes, your audiences go back home and do Google search on your name. If your social credibility stands out, this person will be more impressed. I will touch on this point a little later in this chapter.

4. **Connect** – Be genuine. This is the most important box for making a favourable first impression. This is also where we tend to falter. If I take the example of Ajay who has just bumped into the CEO in the car park area (either by luck or by a planned intervention), he can smile, shake hands and definitely do all the things we discussed above easily. But how does one connect with the CEO? It requires a lot of quick thinking and confidence. Here is what you can do. You can do some basic research on the person in advance through social media or through a mutual friend. It could be the college he attended, or a blog that he has written or something that is common

between you and him like an interest in books etc. A lot of these things can be found from the CEO's LinkedIn profile or through your colleagues who have worked with him. So pick a topic that can act as an ice-breaker and plan a sentence that establishes this connection. Here are some of the ways I typically connect with people I am meeting for the first time

a. A common alma mater
b. A common friend
c. A common interest
d. Something I read about that person in the media
e. A nice thing to say about the person e.g. it is an honour to meet you; I am a big fan of your work (if the person is well known or their work in available in the public domain)

One of the best examples that I have heard of making a lasting impression was from a colleague at Wipro who was invited to a lunch with the CEO in the first week of our joining. His name was Amar. Lunch with the CEO was general practice at Wipro Technologies and was done every year with the new recruits. The invites were sent to a small random group of people by the HR manager. Amar was sitting in that room as well. The CEO was a veteran of the industry and everyone was on their best behaviour. When they all filled our plates and sat down on the table, he asked each one of the new joinies to introduce themselves to him. They went one by one and it was regular, boring stuff. Then Amar's turn came. He introduced himself in a very confidant manner and then asked, 'Sir, would it be okay to share some feedback about our company with you?' All the others were shocked. How could he? They were all young trainees from college and this was the CEO of Wipro he was talking to. It was practically unheard of! The CEO was a seasoned professional and smiled. He said, 'Go on Amar' as he put his spoon down and committed his full attention towards Amar. Amar continued, 'Sir, when I got this job I was on top of the world. But my parents called me up and said that they were disappointed. How could I work for a company that made soaps and oils?' In those days, people knew Wipro as a company that made a famous soap and not as a company that made cutting edge software. There was pin drop silence in the room. Everyone thought that the CEO would get annoyed. But his response was far from it. He laughed heartily, patted Amar on the back and requested the HR manager to setup a meeting with the marketing head of Wipro Technologies later in the day. I heard that the meeting did happen and the feedback was passed on. A day later, Amar got an email from the CEO. 'Dear Amar, your feedback was very valuable. You will hear about our new marketing strategy soon.' Amar has been a fast riser in that company and beyond. I think it is because of his sincere and genuine words and his ability to connect across all levels.

5. **Emotion** – Spread joy. The box of Xtra Emotion can work marvels for your first impression. Leave your audience with a happy or joyful emotion. At a conference where I was a speaker, I met a young student who walked up to me. He had a wonderful infectious smile and exuded confidence. He just gave me his card and on the back of the card, he had written a line from a popular rock song which I also liked. He then said that he was inspired by my talk and felt like mentioning this song to me. I really felt moved and have been in touch with this student since then.

2. Interacting in an informal setup

We all know that in a matrix organization, it helps to know the right people to get your work done. But for this, one must invest time in interacting with them and building a relationship. They could be your seniors, peers, or juniors. So how does one find time in a busy day to interact and connect? And when you do find time, what do you say to them? We can use the AEIOU Xtra E framework in these situations. An important slot that I recommend for all you budding leaders to do these interactions is the lunch and coffee break. I personally built all my networks in these breaks. Let me explain in simple math. Assume you have 20 colleagues that are very important for you to stay in touch with for your work. Let's work with 1 lunch break and 2 coffee breaks. So in a week, you can interact with each of them personally and build good relationships. I try my best to meet new people during the lunch breaks. It gives me a chance to know them better and expand my networks. Most of us tend to sit at a table where we know people. It is our comfort zone. We don't like to sit, let alone eat, with strangers. But think again—here is your chance to build a great relationship in that break. Why miss it? I will highlight the importance of this in the section where I will focus on networking a little later. Let's use the framework and see how we can interact in an informal setup.

1. **Objective** – This is one interaction where I request all of you to have no set objective. Avoid mixing business and friendship. This is the lunch or coffee break. People are looking to recharge their batteries. Help them to have a relaxing time and focus on the interaction alone with no objective. Enjoy meeting a person you don't know and be sincere and genuine in your interaction.

2. **Connect** – A lunch break is short and everyone wants to relax and recharge their batteries. Be very picky with your choices. Stay away from tables that only discuss office gossip and politics. And definitely stay away from negative people or 'energy vampires'. (Orlaaf, 2002). Energy vampires drain you of your energy with their negativity. They can convert you into an energy vampire too as it is contagious. It is best to choose a topic which is common and light. It could be a game, a sport, a movie, or a book that could create an interesting discussion in the group. Be a good listener and participate with genuine interest. Remember, it is not about agreeing or disagreeing. It is about connecting with people and giving each other a good platform to know each other and relax. If you do this right, then you will have many people in your office who would want to sit with you on your table. One can never go wrong with laughter and humour. I had a colleague in one of the companies I worked with who had a huge vault of jokes. He would just pull out one and have the entire group of us eating out of his hands. We would wait for lunch breaks to sit next to him. He was Mr Popular and a great person to be with. Another great way to connect is to be a good listener on the table. Just shut up, let others speak, and fuel the discussion with your active listening skills. Ask open-ended questions and see the magic unfold. I learnt this trick from one of my ex-bosses. He would calmly sit at our lunch table and patiently listen to the topic. Some people would clam up and keep quiet. So he would rope them into the discussion by a simple hook, 'So Rajeev, what do you think about this topic.' Rajeev would start talking and the boss would fuel the discussion with nods and active listening. He would also crack a witty remark or a joke to make everyone comfortable.

But he would not steal the thunder at the lunch table. He would slide into the conversation and keep the focus away from himself. An aunt of mine is fabulous at making conversation. Put her in a room and she will make friends with everyone with her ready smile and willing ear. She will start with the 'So what do you do?' question and then take on a lead from their answer and let them drive the conversation further. Dale Carnegie wrote about this in *How to Win Friends and Influence People*. He says that the best way to win someone in a party is to let them talk and give them a listening ear. (Carnegie, 1936)

3. **Emotion** – Whatever you do, make sure you don't agitate your audiences. It gives a tremendous negative emotion and they will avoid you like the plague.

3. The art of networking with internal and external stakeholders

In one of the workshops I did for my students last year, I asked them to take a blank sheet of paper and fill their overall net worth. I then walked out of the class because I didn't want them to ask questions and crowd their minds. I came back after few minutes and saw everyone eagerly waiting for me. I walked around and read their answers. Most wrote 'XXX rupees in the bank' or a combination of 'money in the bank and a property which could be self-owned or parental'. One student was obviously a big fan of financial modelling and neatly tabulated the assets on one side, subtracted the loans on the other and gave an exact number in the middle. I had expected these answers. I then asked my class to tear those sheets and take fresh ones. I asked them fill their overall net worth that is beyond money or gold or property or bonds or stocks or mutual funds or any financial instrument. I got blank stares. One student raised his hand and asked me, 'What is there besides these to measure my personal worth?' 'Have you considered the value of your personal networks—your friends, connections, colleagues, classmates, alumni, family, cousins, neighbors, and members from clubs/ associations that you are part of?' I asked. 'Assign 1 rupee to casual acquaintances, 100 rupees to your colleagues, 1000 to your classmates and alumni, 10000 to cousins, 1 lakh rupees for every friend who you think you can call for help, and 10 lakh for immediate family members. Basically, the stronger the bonds are, the greater the value of that person in your life.' I saw all of them excitedly filling their sheets, checking their Facebook, LinkedIn, WhatsApp, phone contacts, outlook address books, etc and the maximum wealth that day was around 68 lakhs. And this student was just 21 years old. Imagine the potential if you start nurturing your networks young.

So how does one go about building a professional network? Here are some of the tips you can follow.

1. **Maintain a little black book (LBB)** – Remember *Godfather*? Don Vito Corleone used to maintain a little book in which he would keep score—who is worth giving favours to and what they owed him. Nowadays, technology can step in to help. Some of the best leaders make it a point to enter a note in this LBB every night before sleeping. They capture who they met, the visiting cards they gave, and mentally mapping them as to how they can add value in future.
2. **Invest in people you know** – Once you have a little black book, how do you fill this with details or how does one go about meeting people? Actually, it's very easy. All your friends from school, colleges, community, alumni, neighbourhood, family and friends of family are your

existing networks. Now go beyond them and look into your colleagues or groups you are part of. Make sure you have a cup of coffee or lunch with someone you don't know or want to know better at mutual convenience. Once the coffee or lunch is over, send a polite thank you and add their name and details to the LBB. On weekends, try and sign up for interesting forums where you can meet new people. Ask yourself, what can I offer to my network? Why would they add me to their networks? This is very similar to the pitch we discussed earlier and will look at it here from a networking context. When you meet them, you can apply the AEIOU Xtra E framework as follows.

a. **Objective** – To build your network as measured by having this person's phone, email-id, or any other information that is useful to you in your LBB (it could be your LinkedIn contacts or your phone book, etc). To ensure that the other person also remembers you and adds you to their network. This will happen only when you add value to their network.
b. **U-factor/Connect** – Networking happens in both planned and unplanned events. You might bump into your networks in airports or in conferences. Or you might even plan a meeting with them in their offices or outside at a golf course or a restaurant depending on your objective. The most important part of this box in network context is your ability to add value to their professional lives.
c. **I-factor/Credibility** – Your business card is of great use in this scenario. Exchange them and store them in a place where you can refer to them easily. I also

write notes on the cards that my networks give me, e.g. where I met them, if there something important I want to remember about them, etc.

d. **Emotion** – If you can make your audience remember you and give them an emotion of excitement that adds value to their professional life, you have successfully expanded your network.

3. **Build trust and PNBB** – Once you have started maintaining the LBB and it starts to grow nicely, the third step to fill your professional network bank balance (let's call this PNBB)—fill something to it every day just like how you do with your financial bank. Some of the simplest things you can give to others are a) your time, b) your ear to listen to them, c) knowledge or advice provided they ask for it, d)professional assistance, and e) someone in your LBB who you can connect them to for further help. Remember important events of your networks like birthdays, when they have a baby or an anniversary of their company, etc. Go beyond the designation and the title of people. Get to know them as people and friends. The closer your bonds are, the higher your values of this relationship will be. This is the most important step of building professional networks. In one word, it can be summarized as 'trust'.
4. **Replenish when you encash** – Each network has some value which you have earned over time and effort. Make sure that you replenish it when you redeem it. Thank them for the help they have offered you and offer to help them in return. A negative value means that you lost a precious account. Avoid this at all costs. A negative bank means you lost the trust of that person who was once a friend. And sometimes, they can be more dangerous than having 100 enemies.

5. **Be honest and genuine in networking** – This is a very serious engagement. So make sure you are sincere and do it from your heart with passion. Don't just meet people and tell them that you have been meaning to call them. They can see through your bluff. And the worst is when you call someone and say, 'It's been so long since I spoke to you… And by the way, I need a favour.'

A FEW NOTs TO BE CAREFUL ABOUT

1. Avoid sending an email to a person with your resume unless you know them very well and can trust them. Most young students just shoot emails to senior alumni or executives in companies with their resumes attached hoping for a job.
2. Avoid calling someone directly on the cell phone without prior appointment.
3. Avoid giving contacts of your own networks to others without their prior permission.
4. Avoid being in 'I want a job' mode all the time. Very soon, people get irritated with your constant job requests.
5. Avoid crying on the shoulders of someone who is in your network. Nobody likes having cribbers or energy vampires around.
6. Avoid imposing your own views and thoughts on your members of your networks.

4. A corporate party or a social get together with colleagues

Ask yourself, what do you want the world to know you as? Do they know you as a Mr Sincere in the office by Mr Enfant Terrible in the parties? Just pause and think. Communication outside office, but in an official party, is still communication and may impact how your audience trusts you. Your AEIOU Xtra E framework might crash if you are not careful in these seemingly insignificant but important scenarios. I will give you an example. In one of the corporate parties, a top manager got a little tipsy. When he woke up the next day and came to office, he was called to the room where he was told that a lady colleague had filed a harassment suit against him because of his bad behaviour in the party the previous night. He was shattered and all his 20 years of good work was washed away in one evening. He has now completely vanished from the radar. This scenario is not very different than the ones I discussed above from the framework perspective. I request you to keep the following in mind in a social get together.

1. The laws of communication still hold good here. Nothing changes.
2. Avoid having multiple personalities. Work on having a uniform personality that works both at office and outside office.
3. Be respectful of the culture and laws of the land.
4. No means No. If the lady/gent that you are dancing with that evening says No to your advances, take that very seriously and move on.
5. Feel free to let your hair down but be wary of boundaries.
6. There is nothing unofficial about office parties. So make sure you are on your guard about what to say and when to shut up.

5. *Presence in meetings, conferences*

A conference is a great place to interact and network with industry stakeholders. The AEIOU and Xtra E framework can help you in creating a lasting impression in such a scenario. Here are some tips I would like to give.

1. **Show your presence** – If you are going to a conference, make sure you sit in the front of the room so that the speakers can see you. That is the best way to win their attention and shows that you respect them. The backbencher attitude works in colleges. Quit it in the corporate world. Get noticed and show yourself by being in the front. Once the talk is over, walk up to the speaker and exchange your cards to make a lasting impression and network better. In the lunch and tea breaks, walk around and meet people. Don't waste this opportunity by sitting with people you already know. Every conference has a center of gravity. Make sure you are near that point.
2. **Participate** – In the beginning of the book, I had written about a scenario where an employee asks a question to the CEO in an open house. Asking questions and participating in discussions are wonderful techniques to build your credibility and networks with the audiences. Please know when to shut up as well though. I had given an example of how Chatur had asked an inappropriate question in an open house. Be brief in your question or comment and let others also get a chance. This is not the Group Discussion selection process. You don't have to say something just for the heck of saying it as people do in group discussions. Use the AEIOU Xtra E framework to keep all elements of audience in mind. Before you open your mouth, ask yourself, 'Is this the right place to ask this or should I email or take it offline?'

6. Communicating with media

There is a big difference in interacting with colleagues or customers and communicating with the media, journalists, and members of press. Their job is to communicate a story to their readers or audiences. So indirectly, your audience is their audience. But you have to very careful in giving your messages to them because it can be misinterpreted and misreported, thereby causing you or your company a great harm. If you are going to face the media, you must carefully think through your AEIOU Xtra E framework as below.

1. **Objective** – The objective of your interaction is to give ONLY that information that is approved by your corporate guidelines. Anything beyond that should not be spoken or conveyed.
2. **Connect** – Your audience is not the journalist. It is the readers or viewers of that news. Your job is to represent your company and give a message to them. Connect with them as if they are sitting in front of you. Use eye contact and smile to demonstrate confidence. Audience can sniff a nervous speaker.
3. **Examples or logic** – Support your message by as much data or facts as possible. When you are facing the media, there is no room for opinion. Just give the facts and stick to the script. If you don't know the answer, try and avoid going towards that zone. Stick to the topic that you know and are qualified to talk about.
4. **Attention** – Maintain a smile or an expression that the audience can appreciate. This is all the more important if you are on Television. Dress for the occasion as well.

5. **Credibility** – You need to downplay your personal credibility and represent your company. Try and use 'we' sentences so that it reflects you as a spokesperson of the company.
6. **Emotion** – stay as neutral as possible. Avoid any sentence that can be construed differently. Avoid expressing irritation in your own face and tone.

The Road Ahead...

PERSUASIVE COMMUNICATION CAN BE LEARNT by anyone. One is not born with it. I hope that this book kickstarts your journey to become an effective communicator and become more successful. Here are some suggestions that you could use to continue on this journey of learning further.

JOIN A TOASTMASTERS CLUB

One of the greatest fears many of us face in the corporate world is the fear of speaking in front of an audience. It's called Glossophobia and I have written about this earlier in the book. Here is the bad news. There is no cure for it. And now here is the good news. It can be overcome with practice. Toastmaster clubs offer exactly that. You have a bunch of like-minded people who want to overcome their fears of public speaking and a desire to be successful in life. I joined one in Bangalore and greatly benefitted from it. I started 2 more clubs and still am associated to many of them through my friends and students. I admit that the first few weeks are daunting. But the members are very encouraging and the best part is that they all help each other overcome their fears. They give constructive and timely feedback which fuels further learning. And they are very organized and disciplined—a system that has worked well for over 90 years now and produced some of the world's best leaders. You can visit www.toastmasters.org and find a club near you. Many clubs entertain anyone to walk in and see the meetings in action. The best way is to contact their VP Membership and find out when the next meeting is.

Watch the world's best speakers

We live in the most exciting and connected times. Everything is now available online. Dedicate 20 minutes a day and watch a great speaker on platforms like TED, Youtube, etc. Many of us spend hours in our commute to work. Download these videos on your smart phone and enjoy them during your commute. You can even download just the audio if you want to hear them. All speeches have their transcripts available as well which can be downloaded. I watch a video and read the script simultaneously. I sometimes even take a pen and paper and mark the sentences that fit the AEIOU Xtra E elements of the framework. That way I learn the elements better and sometimes even take few parts of their speeches and use them in different ways in my own.

Observe your colleagues who are good at communication

If you have a colleague or a friend who is good at persuasive communication, observe them more closely. I would even go at length and ask, 'How do you do that?' and see what comes out of it. I have done it many times with my own colleagues and they have given me wonderful tips on how they learnt this skill.

Write

I have firmly believed that writing is the best way to sharpen your thoughts. It is a very intense process and probably a very difficult medium too. But it brings out the best in you. Start with a daily journal and write something. Sign up for creative writing courses if you can. Maintain a blog and be willing to receive feedback from your readers. Keep a pen and a notebook with you at all times.

Read

This is by far the most important request from me to all of you. If you list down the world's top people in any category and then analyse the commonalities in them, I won't be surprised if reading is one of them. A good book is worth 3 months of wisdom of one's life. So if you read 100 books in 5 years, you have gained 300 months or 25 years of wisdom in your life. Now that is huge return on your investment. Moreover, you can use this wisdom in your AEIOU Xtra E framework as well.

Watch movies

Movies are a great source of learning. You can learn how to use emotions, how to draft sentences, and also improve your diction. I use snippets of movies as stories in my talks and it greatly entertains my audiences. If you have studied in a vernacular medium, then English movies with subtitles can greatly help you speak the language better. It can be straining but worth it ultimately.

Be social. Meet new people

Overcome your shyness. Make sure you meet new people and interact with them. Build your confidence and networks. Observe how they meet and greet each other. It will help you become a social person which will show in your communication as well.

Practice, practice, practice

In all my classes, I start by saying, 'Communication cannot be learnt by reading the subject alone. It must be practiced.' Make practice as a part of your communication process. Do dry runs in front of a mirror or in front of your friends. There is no harm in trying and failing. Take risks and explore newer ways of saying the same message. Beyond a point, everything is worthless if you don't practice this skill in the real world.

The art of communication is the language of leadership. So if you want to become successful leaders, start investing on in skill. There is no age for learning. Start today!

Bibliography

Chapter 1

Anonymous, 2013. *Diplo Learning Corner.* [Online]

Available at: http://diplolearn.wordpress.com/2013/06/08/the-rule-of-conflicts/.

Barrett, D. J., 2006. Leadership Communication: A Communication Approach for Senior-Level Managers. In: *Handbook of Business Strategy.* s.l.: Emerald Group Publishing, pp. 385-390.

Colorado, C. R. C. U. o., 2005. *International Online Training Program On Intractable Conflict.* [Online]

Available at: http://www.colorado.edu/conflict/peace/!overlay_problems.htm#commprob.

Fluto, F. J., 1999. Walking the Talk: The Relationship Between Leadership and Communication Competence. *Journal of Leadership & Organizational Studies,* Volume 6, pp. 86-97.

R.S., A., 2014. *The Hindu.* [Online]

Available at: http://www.thehindu.com/features/magazine/section-377-the-way-forward/article5740242.ece.

Chapter 2

Black, D. L., 2014. *The creative process of an Oscar-winning screenwriter.* [Online]

Available at: http://sploid.gizmodo.com/the-insane-creative-process-of-an-oscar-winning-screenw-1601624702?utm_campaign=socialflow_gizmodo_facebook&utm_source=gizmodo_facebook&utm_medium=socialflow.

Cutler, K.-M., 2013. *A Dongle Joke That Spiraled Way Out Of Control.* [Online]

Available at: http://techcrunch.com/2013/03/21/a-dongle-joke-that-spiraled-way-out-of-control/.

Ferro, S., 2014. *Why You Should Read More Novels.* [Online]

Available at: http://www.fastcodesign.com/3024259/asides/why-you-should-read-more-novels?partner=rss.

Gandhi, M. K., 1952. Selected works of Mahatma Gandhi. In: *Mahatama.* s.l.:s.n., pp. 28-30.

Kennedy Forum Channel on Youtube, J. F., 2013. *The Language and Legacy of Presidential Speechwriting.* [Online]

Available at: http://www.youtube.com/watch?v=kaT_9ULzf2w.

Rogers, C. R. & Roethlisberger, F. J., 1991. Barriers and gateways to communication. *Harvard Business Review,* 69(6), pp. 105-111.

Sunstrom, L., 2013. *www.lifehack.org.* [Online]

Available at: http://www.lifehack.org/articles/communication/are-you-suffering-from-the-curse-knowledge.html.

Youtube Malala, Y., 2013. *YouTube.* [Online]

Availableat: http://www.youtube.com/watch?v=QRh_30C8l6Y.

Chapter 3

Ahmed, Z., Shields, F., White, R. & Wilbert, J., 2010. The link between frontline leadership and organizational performance. *Journal of Organizational Culture,* Volume 14, pp. 107-120.

Barrett, D. J., 2006. Leadership Communication:A Communication Approach for Senior-Level Managers. In: *Handbook of Business Strategy.* s.l.: Emerald Group Publishing, pp. 385-390.

Bharadwaj, S., 2013. *http://www.shreyasbharadwaj.com/curious-minds/14-vidya-64-kala.* [Online]

Available at: http://www.shreyasbharadwaj.com.

Eccles, R., Noharia, N. & Berkeley, J., 1992. *Beyond the Hype: Rediscovering the Essence of Management.* Boston: Harvard School Press.

Essence, 2014. *Essence.com.* [Online]

Available at: http://www.essence.com/2014/02/27/lupita-nyongo-delivers-moving-black-women-hollywood-acceptance-speech/.

Essence, 2014. *Lupita Nyong'o Delivers Moving 'Black Women in Hollywood' Acceptance Speech.* [Online]

Available at: http://www.essence.com/2014/02/27/lupita-nyongo-delivers-moving-black-women-hollywood-acceptance-speech/.

Fluto, F. J., 1999. Walking the Talk: The Relationship Between Leadership and Communication Competence. *Journal of Leadership & Organizational Studies,* Volume 6, pp. 86-97.

Gladwell, M., 2009. *The 10,000 Hour Rule.* [Online]

Available at: http://gladwell.com/outliers/the-10000-hour-rule/.

GMAC, 2014. *Corporate Recruiters Survey,* s.l.: GMAC.

Jain, N. & Mukherji, S., 2009. Communicating a holistic perspective to the world. *Leadership & Organization Development Journal,* 30(5), pp. 435-454.

Kennedy, G. A., 1991. *On Rhetoric: A Theory of Civil Discourse.* s.l.: Oxford English Press.

Mintzberg, H., 1973. *The nature of managerial work.* s.l.: Harper & Row.

Nair, R. B., 2013. *Manwatching Mister Modi.* [Online]

Available at: http://www.outlookindia.com/article/Manwatching-Mister-Modi/286143.

Vries, R. E. d., Bakker-Pieper, A. & Oostenveld, W., 2009. *Leadership= Communication? The Relations of Leaders' Communication Styles with Leadership Styles, Knowledge Sharing and Leadership Outcomes.* [Online]

Available at: www.springlink.com.

YoutubeKejriwal, 2013. *Youtube.* [Online]

Available at: http://www.youtube.com/watch?v=K8BDanwg E6E.

CHAPTER 4

Iridium, 2010. *Wikipedia.* [Online]

Available at: http://en.wikipedia.org/wiki/Iridium_satellite_constellation.

Kotler, P., 1967. *Marketing Mix.* [Online]

Available at: http://en.wikipedia.org/wiki/Marketing_mix.

Mehrabian, A., 1972. *Non-Verbal Communication.* s.l.: Aldine-Atherton.

Obama, B., 2012. *The Official Whitehouse of USA webpage.* [Online]

Available at: http://www.whitehouse.gov/blog/2012/12/14/president-obama-speaks-shooting-connecticut

Philip Kotler, G. A., 2013. Marketing segmentation. In: *Principles of Marketing.* s.l.: Prentice Hall.

Straker, D., 2010. *ChanginMinds.Org.* [Online]

Available at: http://changingminds.org/explanations/behaviors/body_language/mehrabian.htm.

Chapter 5

VRod, H., 2003. *YouTube.* [Online]

Available at: http://www.youtube.com/watch?v=cWPX-nFDrfM.

Yousuf, M., 2013. *The Independent.* [Online]

Available at: http://www.independent.co.uk/news/world/asia/the-full-text-malala-yousafzai-delivers-defiant-riposte-to-taliban-militants-with-speech-to-the-un-general-assembly-8706606.html

Chapter 6

Brooks, C., 2012. *Yahoo Online.* [Online]

Available at: http://news.yahoo.com/yahoo-ceo-not-alone-7-execs-busted-resume-160624891.html.

Budzowski, B., n.d. *incrediblemessages.com.* [Online]

Available at: http://www.incrediblemessages.com/pdf/articles/White-Paper-Credibility-Need-to-Care.pdf.

Cialdini, R., 2001. Harnessing the science of persuasion. *HBR.*

Hewlett, S. A., 2014. *HBR Blogs.* [Online]

Available at: http://blogs.hbr.org/2014/04/as-you-start-your-career-focus-on-people-skills/.

Obama, B., 2009. *ObamaSpeeches.* [Online]

Available at: http://obamaspeeches.com/.

Souza, P., 2010. *The Rise of Barack Obama.* [Online]

Available at: http://www.petesouza.com/gallery.html?gallery=The+Rise+of+Barack+Obama&folio=Image%20Galleries#/0.

TED, 2014. *Ted.com.* [Online]

Available at: www.ted.com.

Chapter 7

Aiyar, M. S., 2012. *The Hindu.* [Online]

Available at: http://www.thehindu.com/opinion/lead/food-security-the-cup-of-tantalus/article3304642.ece.

APMYY, 2014. *Funsterz.* [Online]

Available at: http://funsterz.com/2014/06/26/mind-blowing-facts-about-india-16-photos/.

Denning, S., 2004. Telling Tales. *Harvard Business Review,* 82(5), pp. 122-129.

Dlugan, A., 2012. *Six Minutes.* [Online]

Available at: http://sixminutes.dlugan.com/speech-analysis-dream-martin-luther-king/.

Elop, S., 2011. *Wall Street Journel.* [Online]

Available at: http://blogs.wsj.com/tech-europe/2011/02/09/full-text-nokia-ceo-stephen-elops-burning-platform-memo/.

Kennedy, G. A., 1991. *On Rhetoric:A theory of civic discourse.* s.l.:Oxford university press.

King, M. L., 1963. *American Rhetoric.* [Online]

Available at: http://www.americanrhetoric.com/speeches/mlkihaveadream.htm.

Krugman, P., 2011. *NY Times.* [Online]

Available at: http://www.nytimes.com/2011/09/19/opinion/economic-bleeding-cure.html?module=Search&mabReward=relbias%3Ar%2C[%22RI%3A5%22%2C%22RI%3A12%22].

Leonard Susskind: My friend Richard Feynman. 2011. [Film] Directed by TED. USA: TED.

Mascarenhas, H., 2014. *15 Powerful Quotes From the World's Most Humble President.* [Online]

Available at: http://mic.com/articles/92369/15-powerful-quotes-from-the-world-s-most-humble-president.

Pittsburg, U. o., 2007. *Speaking in the disciplines.* [Online]

Available at: http://www.speaking.pitt.edu/student/public-speaking/reasoning.html.

PoolCalculator, 2014. *Havuz.org.* unknown: http://www.havuz.org/pool-calculators.htm#pool_volume.

Rapp, C., 2010. *Stanford Encyclopedia of Philosophy.* [Online]

Available at: http://plato.stanford.edu/entries/aristotle-rhetoric/.

Rosling, H., 2010. *YouTube.* [Online]

Available at: http://www.youtube.com/watch?v=fTznEIZRkLg&list=PLSrgd_ElrrXegdtDHPmUzrzLpwZ2dSYKg

Sheen, M., 2010. *WeDay.com.* [Online]

Available at: http://www.weday.com/we-day-events/past-events/national-we-day/

Steve Jobs Commencement speech at Stanford. 2005. [Film] USA: Youtube.

TED.com, 2005. *Hans Rosling Speaker Profile.* [Online]

Available at: http://www.ted.com/speakers/hans_rosling

Tindale, C. W., 2004. *Rhetorical Argumentation: Principles of Theory and Practice.* s.l.:Sage Publications.

UCMAS, 2007. *Left Brain Vs Right Brain.* [Online]

Available at: http://www.ucmas.in/our-programs/whole-brain-development/left-brain-vs-right-brain/

Wildrich, L., 2012. *The Science of Storytelling: Why Telling a Story is the Most Powerful Way to Activate Our Brains.* [Online]

Available at: http://lifehacker.com/5965703/the-science-of-storytelling-why-telling-a-story-is-the-most-powerful-way-to-activate-our-brains.

Yarrow, J., 2011. *Business Insider.* [Online]

Available at: http://www.businessinsider.com/the-full-text-of-steve-jobs-stanford-commencement-speech-2011-10?IR=T.

Chapter 8

Carnegie, D., 1936. *How to win friends and influence people.* USA: Simon and Schuster.

Conger, J. A., 1998. The necessary art of persuasion. *Harvard Business Review,* 76(3), pp. 84-95.

Modi, N., 2014. *NarendraModi.in.* [Online]

Available at: http://www.narendramodi.in/text-speech-of-pm-narendra-modi-at-pslv-c23-launch-at-sriharikota/.

Nadella, S., 2014. *Microsoft.com.* [Online]

Available at: http://www.microsoft.com/en-us/news/press/2014/feb14/02-04mail2.aspx.

Swades, 2004. *YouTube.* [Online]

Available at: https://www.youtube.com/watch?v=7Eaaj0lP2F0.

Swaraj, S., 2014. *The Hindu.* [Online]

Available at: http://m.thehindubusinessline.com/news/in-chaste-urdu-sushma-charms-the-haj-congregation/article6141596.ece/.

CHAPTER 9

Carnegie, D., 1936. *How to win friends and influence people.* USA: Simon and Schuster .

Foster, C., 2014. *Satchi & Satchi.* [Online]

Available at: http://www.saatchiasiapacific.com/category/thought-leadership/page/2/.

Marr, B., 2014. *LinkedIN.* [Online]

Available at: https://www.linkedin.com/today/post/article/20140707061900-64875646-the-15-biggest-body-language-mistakes-to-watch-out-for?trk=tod-home-art-list-small_3.

Perry, R., 1981. *NobelPrize.Org.* [Online]

Available at: http://www.nobelprize.org/nobel_prizes/medicine/laureates/1981/sperry-facts.html.

Rock, M., 2014. *Hey, Parents. What That IPad Is Doing to Your Kid Is Kind of Shocking..* [Online]

Available at: http://m.2machines.com/articles/181304.html.

Treasure, J., 2013. *TED.com.* [Online]

Available at: http://www.ted.com/talks/julian_treasure_how_to_speak_so_that_people_want_to_listen#t-482261.

Weinschenk, S., 2012. *100 Things Every Presenter Needs To Know About People.* California: Newriders.

Willis, J. & Todorov, A., 2006. *Princeton University.* [Online]

Available at: http://www.princeton.edu/main/news/archive/S15/62/69K40/index.xml?section=topstories.

Woodmore, S., 2011. *Wikipedia.* [Online]

Available at: en.wikipedia.org/wiki/Words_per_minute#References.

CHAPTER 10

Adam D. I. Kramer, J. E. G. J. T. H., 2014. Experimental evidence of massive-scale emotional contagion through social networks. *PNAS,* Issue 24.

Bechara, A., 2004. The role of emotion in decision-making: Evidence from neurological patients with orbitofrontal damage. *Brain and Cognition,* 55(1), pp. 30-40.

Ekman, P., 2003. *Emotions Revealed.* second ed. New York: Owl Books.

Lindstorm, M., 2008. *Buyology: Truth and Lies About Why We Buy.* First Paperback ed. New York: Broadway.

Lumet, S., 1957. *IMDB.* [Online]

Available at: http://www.imdb.com/title/tt0050083/.

Maclean, P., 1960. *Triune Brain.* [Online] Available at: http://en.wikipedia.org/wiki/Triune_brain

Martino, B. D., 2006. *USA Today.* [Online] Available at: http://usatoday30.usatoday.com/tech/science/discoveries/2006-08-06-brain-study_x.htm.

Suzuki, S., 1992. *Youtube.* [Online]

Available at: http://www.youtube.com/watch?v=IqrBzuOwGqQ.

Swaraj, S., 2011. *Youtube.* [Online] Available at: http://www.youtube.com/watch?v=9b8IpXdWcQM.

CHAPTER 11

Cahn, S. & Cahn, V., 2013. *Chronicle of higher education.* [Online]

Available at: http://chronicle.com/article/Polishing-Your-Prose-Word-by/137327/.

Dayley, T., 2013. *Fstoppers.* [Online]

Available at: http://fstoppers.com/post-production/colgates-clever-advertising-campaign-4002.

Favreau, J., 2013. *Youtube.* [Online]

Available at: http://www.youtube.com/watch?v=kaT_9ULzf2w.

Steven Cahn, V. C., 2013. *Polishing your prose.* New York: Columbia Univerity Press.

CHAPTER 12

Martin, C., 2013. *Why Should We Hire You?*. [Online]

Available at: http://career-advice.monster.com/job-interview/interview-questions/why-should-we-hire-you/article.aspx.

Obama, B., 2012. *WhiteHouse.gov.* [Online]

Available at: http://www.whitehouse.gov/blog/2012/12/14/president-obama-speaks-shooting-connecticut.

Pattanaik, D., 2010. *How to communicate tactfully with your boss.* [Online]

Available at: http://articles.economictimes.indiatimes.com/2010-02-12/news/28399452_1_king-nathan-bad-light.

Soundarajan, R., 2014. Flipkart Apology: A gold standard indeed. [Online]

Available at: http://www.afaqs.com/all/news/case_studies/reports/331/FLASH/index.htm

Wodtke, C., 2014. *Tell Me A Little Bit About Yourself.* [Online]

Available at: https://www.linkedin.com/today/post/article/20140617162134-93094-tell-me-a-little-bit-about-yourself.

CHAPTER 13

Coolsen, F., 1947. Pioneers in the Development of Advertising. *Journal of Marketing*, 12(1), p. 82.

Elsbach, K. D., 2003. How to pitch a brilliant idea. *Harvard Business Review*.

Finder, J., 2003. *What's a Hook? The Art of the Pitch.* [Online]

Available at: http://www.josephfinder.com/writers/tips/whats-a-hook-the-art-of-the-pitch.

Wikipedia, n.d. *AIDA(marketing).* [Online]

Available at: http://en.wikipedia.org/wiki/AIDA_%28 marketing%29.

Chapter 14

Carnegie, D., 1936. *How to win friends and influence people.* USA: Simon and Schuster .

Haden, J., 2014. *Hugh Jackman Hailed Me a Cab: The Power of Lasting Impressions.* [Online]

Available at: http://www.linkedin.com/today/post/article/20140724122346-20017018-hugh-jackman-hailed-me-a-cab-the-power-of-lasting-impressions?trk=mp-details-rc.

Orlaaf, J., 2002. *O Magazine Energy Vampires.* [Online]

Available at: http://www.oprah.com/omagazine/Protect-Yourself-from-Energy-Vampires.

Uleman, J., n.d. *American Psychological Association.* [Online]

Available at: http://www.apa.org/gradpsych/2012/11/first-impressions.aspx.

Acknowledgements

What to Say and When to Shut Up is a dream come true for me. I started teaching the art of influencing and communicating effectively in 1999 as a hobby during weekends. The hobby slowly became my passion and I started to do workshops in the companies I worked for in my spare time. I finally decided to take the *Plunnge* in 2008 and teach this subject full time. While teaching, I discovered my love for writing. Just as I can teach for hours without getting tired, similarly I could shut myself in my room for hours and write. A written word has a lot more impact on the world. And my first 2 books, *Plunnge* and *Seek*, helped me reach out to audiences far and wide.

This book is my third and totally different from the first two. It is the core focus of my academic career that I have decided for myself. In 2011, I signed up for a PhD program which fuelled my passion for this topic even further. I read various books and academic papers written on this topic by experts and professionals from the western world. In many countries this subject is given a lot of importance and it is taught as early as junior school.

So what is this book about? We all look up to leaders like Gandhi, Modi, Jobs, Malala and many more. Their words and messages inspire us. I started writing this book based on a very fundamental question—How did these leaders create those messages and influence their audiences? And finally—Why can't I do the same?

Slowly a pattern emerged and the contours of the AEIOU Xtra E framework took shape. I knew that I had to take this simple framework to everyone who is interested to learn this subject and become a persuasive communicator. I wish that this book also brings more focus on this subject in all schools and colleges. It is a known fact that the top need of the industry today is skilled manpower. Communication and persuasive skills would rank very high in that aspect. This book is my way to help my country in that objective.

This book wouldn't have been possible without support from all of my colleagues, teachers and alumni of IIM Bangalore, my research guides from Cardiff Metropolitan University Professor Eleri Jones and Dr Mukul Madahar, and my students from all the programmes I have taught at and from my friends in the industry. Anamika Chakravarty, Sharda Agarwal, Priyanka Niwas, Sapna Agarwal, Amitabha Saha Roy, Isha Suman, Sathish Hariharan, Savitha S.R., Pushpapreeya, Shaleen Sharma, Gayatri Balaji, Aruna Gopakumar, Prahlad Agiwal, and Bina Soundarajan sent me excellent cases which I have curated as exercises or examples for the book. Special thanks to Gayatri Nair who also helped me in the first 2 books that I wrote and continues to be an honest and fearless critic of my work.

A big shout out to my lovely team—Radhika, Anindita, Caroline and Milee from Random House India. Thank you for your excellent support and patience.

My Mom and Dad for their blessings. My wife for being there for me and supporting my passion of teaching and writing. A great help came from my 11 year old son who took charge of babysitting his little sister and kept her entertained so I could write.

Last not least, my God, philosopher, and guide—Krishna. Thank you for giving me an opportunity to do your work.

A Note on the Author

Rakesh Godhwani calls himself a nobody. After spending amazing formative years in great organizations in the high-tech space like Wipro, Intel and Qualcomm—doing different roles in sales, product marketing and business development—Rakesh realized that his passion lay in helping others reach their maximum potential and fulfil their dreams.

Rakesh currently heads IIM Bangalore Alumni Association, coaches entrepreneurs and leaders in the hi-tech sector, teaches Managerial Communication and Communication for Leaders at IIM Bangalore, does yoga, cycles his way to work, earns a fraction of what he used to but lives a million times better. Rakesh's first book *Plunnge* was released in July, 2011. More details can be found on www.plunnge.com or www.facebook.com/plunnge. His second book *Seek: Finding Your True Calling* was published by Random House India in 2013.

He is an alumnus of KREC (now NITK) Surathkal, class of 1997 and of IIM Bangalore PGSEM, class of 2004. Rakesh is currently pursuing his PhD from Cardiff Metropolitan University which is expected to finish in 2015.

You can follow his blog at rakeshgodhwani.wordpress.com.